U0558835

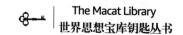
The Macat Library
世界思想宝库钥匙丛书

解析威廉·詹姆斯

《心理学原理》

AN ANALYSIS OF
WILLIAM JAMES'S
THE PRINCIPLES OF PSYCHOLOGY

The Macat Team ◎ 著

叶娟 ◎ 译

上海外语教育出版社
外教社 SHANGHAI FOREIGN LANGUAGE EDUCTION PRESS

目　录

CONTENTS

引言

要点

- 威廉·詹姆斯（1842—1910），美国心理学家、哲学家和生理学家。"心理学"*是研究人类思维和行为的科学；"生理学"*是研究身体器官性质和功能的科学。
- 《心理学原理》（1890）旨在将关乎人类思想和行为的哲学思想引入实证*（基于证据的）领域。
- 尽管《心理学原理》是心理学领域的基础读物，但它的影响在现今许多不同学科中仍有体现，包括艺术和文学。

威廉·詹姆斯其人

威廉·詹姆斯，1842年生于美国纽约，《心理学原理》（1890）的作者。他的弟弟亨利·詹姆斯*是著名的美国小说家。兄弟二人关系亲近，与另外两个弟弟和一个妹妹一起长大，他们在孩童时期都获得了良好的家庭教育。出色的詹姆斯家族男孩子们明白，"如果一个人不质疑也不发表意见，他不仅是在逃避课业，也是在推卸辨别是非的责任。"[1]因此，亨利和威廉都以艺术和技巧为核心，用心、机敏地专注于他们各自所选择的领域（分别是文学和心理学）。

威廉·詹姆斯十几岁时选择到瑞士的日内瓦、法国的巴黎和滨海布洛涅学习科学。1858年，他回到美国，在罗得岛的纽波特学习绘画。就这样，詹姆斯一边在欧洲学习科学，一边在纽波特学习绘画。1861年，他决定进入哈佛大学学习医学。四年后，他和老师——瑞士生物学家吉恩·路易斯·阿加西斯*一起进行了亚马孙河*的考察。在接下来的几年里，他有幸投入德国著名医生威廉·冯特*和赫尔曼·冯·亥姆霍兹*门下，当时这两人刚刚投身于心理学领域，这也激发了詹姆斯对这门学科的兴趣。詹姆斯在哈佛完成学业后，于 1874 年建立了美国第一个心理学实验室，并于 1878 年开始撰写《心理学原理》。

整个 19 世纪 80 年代，詹姆斯一直专注于《心理学原理》的写作，并于 1890 年将其出版。与此同时，他也在哈佛教授心理学和哲学。《心理学原理》是他最重要的著作。在之后的众多作品中，詹姆斯也就同样的生理和心理方面的问题进行了探讨，其中包括《信仰的意志和通俗哲学论文集》（1897）、《宗教经验种种》，以及后期作品《实用主义》（1907）、《多元的宇宙》（1909）和《彻底的经验主义》（1912）。1910 年，詹姆斯去世。

《心理学原理》的主要内容

在《心理学原理》中，詹姆斯试图将心理学确立为一门自然科学，他认为心理学是对"意识状态本身的描述和解释"。[2] 他试图用内省 * 的方法（即研究人的内心并描绘出我们在内心的发现）来探究人类身心之间的关系，特别是人类的大脑结构。[3]

詹姆斯试图将原本孤立的科学风格统一为一个整体；作为一名哲学家和内科医生，他还尝试将哲学思想与生物学和医学联系起来，因此《心理学原理》在心理学史上仍具有十分重要的意义。

"意识流" * 是詹姆斯在《心理学原理》中阐述的最重要概念之一，是他自创的一个概念。他认为所有的思想都是一个接一个发生，并且是相互联系的，因此可用"流"的比喻来说明这个概念。詹姆斯认为，这种持续不断的思想流**是**一种意识——不断的思考、自我反省、创新、感觉等等，全都混杂在一起。其他心理学家则倾向于将心理状态分成不同的部分，例如，他们可能会将一个黄色的球看作一种颜色、一种形状或一个概念，而不是一个整体的"概念"。

詹姆斯还认为，人的生理和心理是以独特的方式相互联系起来的。他认为，人的情绪和习惯是心理、大脑和身体之间相互作用的结果，而不仅仅是一种心理状态。例如，他认为情绪是由身体的变化引发的，正如心理感知的那样——比如心跳加速和脸红。詹姆斯也相信，如果人们强迫自己以某种方式行事，他们就能控制自己的情绪。

在《心理学原理》的核心章节中，詹姆斯试图解释什么是心理与心理的内部运作方式。在这方面，他与早期哲学家更为机械的思想形成了对比，如18世纪的苏格兰哲学家大卫·休谟*以及他的追随者德国的伊曼努尔·康德*。休谟和康德试图用运算的方式从完全理性的角度去理解心理，而詹姆斯则寻求对人类经验更丰富的解读。通过观察人类的行为，他想让心理学，连同它所有的不完美和人性部分，成为一门不同于哲学的学科。

《心理学原理》的学术价值

即使在出版的125年后，《心理学原理》结合哲学、生理学和心理学进行研究的方法依然影响着我们的思维方式。毫无疑问，这对于心理学学科仍至关重要，也是人类思想史上的一个里程碑。《心理学原理》使心理学成为一门有别于生物学或化学的独立科学。19世纪末美国和欧洲探索心理学的兴趣日益增长，这本书起了主要的推动作用。

《心理学原理》的影响力如此之大，詹姆斯也因此被后人敬仰为"美国心理学之父"。尽管心理学及其相关领域在20世纪取得了长足的进步，学生们也不再把《心理学原理》当作教科书，但它对心理学学科的影响仍是不可否认的。这部作品在思想学史上有着举足轻重的作用。

除了心理学之外，它还对哲学学科产生了影响，促进了实用主义 *（一种以哲学探究的实际应用为主的方法）和现象学 *（粗略地说，探究知觉和经验在意识形成和表达中的性质和作用）运动。詹姆斯的《心理学原理》影响了美国和欧洲几代的学者，包括美国思想家约翰·杜威 *，英国哲学家和社会活动家伯特兰· 罗素 *，奥地利裔英国语言哲学家、精神哲学家路德维希·维特根斯坦 * 等。詹姆斯在《心理学原理》中对内省性和艺术性的深刻见解也对现代艺术和文学产生了影响。艺术家们，尤其是作家们，被詹姆斯提到的心理概念深深吸引。也许最有意义的是，詹姆斯提出的"意识流"概念，对于理解现代主义作家如何创作长篇和短篇小说变得非常重要（"现代主义" * 是 20 世纪初艺术和建筑领域的一场挑战传统的运动）。事实上，詹姆斯提出的"意识流"作为文学手段比其作为心理学概念更为人所熟知。一些作家都在他们的作品中使用了此概念的变体，如詹姆斯·乔伊斯 * 的《尤利西斯》（1922）、弗吉尼亚·伍尔芙 * 的《海浪》（1931），以及马塞尔· 普鲁斯特 * 的《追忆逝水年华》（1913—1927）。

《心理学原理》无疑对思想界产生了深远影响。

---

1. 尤金·泰勒："哦，那些了不起的詹姆斯男孩！"，《今日心理学》，2011 年 12 月 15 日，登录日期 2015 年 12 月 17 日，https://www.psychologytoday.com/articles/

199503/oh-those-fabulous-james-boys。

2. 威廉·詹姆斯:《心理学简编》,马萨诸塞州坎布里奇和伦敦:哈佛大学出版社,1984年,第1页。

3. 威廉·詹姆斯:《心理学原理》(第1—2卷),马萨诸塞州坎布里奇:哈佛大学出版社,1981年,第185页。

第一部分：学术渊源

1 作者生平与历史背景

要点 ⚯━

- 《心理学原理》一直是西方心理学（研究人类心理与行为的科学）史上非常重要的著作。

- 詹姆斯在纽约的童年、青春期和成年时期都跟随父亲受到了基督教运动斯韦登堡主义*的影响，此外，他还受到其父母都市知性理念的影响。

- 至19世纪末，许多思想家（如詹姆斯）似乎越来越清楚地认识到，哲学等传统学科，甚至生物学等相对较新的科学都不能解释人的心理。

为何要读这部著作？

在1890年版《心理学原理》中，威廉·詹姆斯巩固了心理学这门新学科的地位，使其成为人文科学和自然科学之间的桥梁。虽然詹姆斯已经是一个众所周知的名字，但1890年版《心理学原理》的出版使他在心理学这一新兴领域的地位更加显赫。

然而，詹姆斯的影响也不仅限于心理学领域。他提出"意识流"的概念，认为意识是通过源源不断的思考、观察和回忆形成的。此后，"意识流"的概念在文学语境中被广泛使用。20世纪早期的著名作家，爱尔兰的詹姆斯·乔伊斯、英国的弗吉尼亚·伍尔芙，以及法国的马塞尔·普鲁斯特分别在他们的作品中使用了这一概念。曾有位作家评论说，"据分析，一定程度上使用意识流手法的小说往往会将一个或多个人物的意识作为其重要主旨……所描绘的意识起到了荧幕的作用，使小说中的素材在荧幕上一一呈现出来。"[1]

《心理学原理》对于西方心理学的影响不可估量，评论家们誉其为詹姆斯的核心著作。当代学者公开赞扬詹姆斯是 19 世纪末 20 世纪初最具影响力的美国哲学家和心理学家，这也显示出其在历史上无与伦比的重要性。[2]

> "人类的大脑容量大约有 1 350 立方厘米，它是世界上最复杂的有机结构。"
>
> ——大卫·M. 布斯：《进化心理学基础》

作者生平

威廉·詹姆斯 1842 年 1 月 11 日出生于美国纽约市。他的父亲十分富有，是瑞典科学家和宗教神秘主义者伊曼纽尔·斯韦登堡创立的宗教运动的追随者，他的母亲是纽约上层社会精英。由于家族经常在欧洲与美国两处奔波，詹姆斯的早期教育主要来自家庭教师和私立学校。这种奔波的生活也使得年幼的詹姆斯感到孤独，没有归属感。

1861 年詹姆斯进入哈佛大学劳伦斯科学学院，1864 年开始在哈佛医学院学习。在结束了亚马孙的学术考察并在欧洲度过了一段时间之后，1866 年詹姆斯回到哈佛大学继续他的学业，并于 1869 年获得了哈佛大学医学学位。

1868 年在欧洲时，詹姆斯获得了与威廉·冯特和赫尔曼·冯·亥姆霍兹一起做研究的机会，这两位德国医生都对人类的心理感兴趣，这也激发了詹姆斯对心理学的关注。[3] 1872 年，詹姆斯开始在哈佛大学教授本科课程比较生理学。直到 1874

年，他不仅教解剖学和生理学，还教心理学。1878 年，他与爱丽丝·豪·吉本斯结婚。两年后，学校任命詹姆斯为哲学助理教授。

19 世纪 80 年代，詹姆斯所从事的心理学和哲学教学工作为《心理学原理》的写作提供了依据。1890 年，詹姆斯的最重要著作《心理学原理》终于完成。他在之后的作品中又多次讨论了许多相同的问题，尤其是生理和心理之间的关系，比如《信仰的意志和通俗哲学论文集》(1897)、《宗教经验种种》(基于 1901—1902 年发表的演讲)，以及后期作品如《实用主义》(1907)、《多元的宇宙》(1909) 和《彻底的经验主义》(1912)。

创作背景

对詹姆斯而言，第二次工业革命 * 中发生的一些历史事件对《心理学原理》产生了重要影响。工业化之前，欧洲是农业经济。人们居住在村庄里，种植足够的粮食作物自给自足，并向土地拥有者交租纳税。始于 18 世纪的第一次工业革命促进了西欧经济和社会的转型。随着新的生产方式的出现，例如使用蒸汽机生产商品，人们的生活方式也随之改变。人们开始在城市里打工，而这些城市也越来越多地由蒸汽火车和蒸汽船连接起来。为了私人利益而进行贸易并发展工业的资本主义 *，成为西方的主要经济体系。

第二次工业革命始于詹姆斯生活的时代，即 19 世纪末。第一次工业革命将生产活动集中在几个中心，使人们更容易获得机器运转所需的煤。但是，电力的发明使得工厂几乎可以在发达国家的任何地方出现。于是，大量的人从农场搬到城市，在城市之间流动。他们远离传统的生活环境和社会支撑架构，进入到不熟悉的环境当中。这种离群索居 * 的生活状态深深地困扰着工人阶级，只有从心理层面出发才能理解他们的困境，而詹姆斯等学者试图从心理角度来解释到底发生了什么。

在《心理学原理》中，在公正看待人类体验复杂性的前提下，詹姆斯试图揭开人类经验的神秘面纱。同时，他支持将心理学作为一门科学学科在美国创立。

---

1. 罗伯特·汉弗莱：《现代小说意识流：对詹姆斯·乔伊斯、弗吉尼亚·伍尔芙、多萝西·理查森、威廉·福克纳等人的研究》，伯克利：加州大学出版社，1968年，第 2 页。

2. 戴维·巴斯：《进化心理学：心理的新科学》，波士顿：培生出版社，2008 年，第 2—35 页。

3. 斯蒂芬妮·L. 霍金斯："威廉·詹姆斯、古斯塔夫·费希尔和早期的心理物理学"，《生理学前沿》，2011 年第 2 期，第 68 页，登录日期 2016 年 2 月，doi:10.3389/fphys.2011.00068。

2 学术背景

要点 ⚷—

- 《心理学原理》是一部跨学科巨著，它结合了心理学、哲学和生理学。

- 詹姆斯的作品可以被认为是古希腊学者和文艺复兴*时期哲学家（如法国思想家笛卡尔*及其追随者）的一系列研究成果的升华（文艺复兴指，中世纪之后，欧洲兴起的一股复兴古希腊、古罗马时代艺术和建筑样式的浪潮）。

- 除了心理学和哲学，詹姆斯也深受英国博物学家查尔斯·达尔文*的影响，而达尔文的作品对现代进化论的发展至关重要。

著作语境

在威廉·詹姆斯撰写《心理学原理》之前，学者们就对心理学的学科地位争论不休。总的来说，他们认为这门学科介于科学和哲学之间，是一门探究型学科，"以方法多样，话题有趣，假设人性为特征"。[1]人们认为这门学科不涉及四肢，也未必关于**大脑**，而是人的心理。许多人认为这门学科与人们的精神生活——思想、动机——息息相关。

这样一个关于心理的哲学概念可以作为一门科学来研究吗？毕竟，科学是以实证研究数据，即观察得出的可证信息为基础的。那么，如何去观察一个人的"心理"呢？"心理"实际上在身体的什么地方呢？当詹姆斯写《心理学原理》时，学者们开始逐渐接受心理学是一门研究心理和灵魂的科学，但是他们仍然无法确定心理学的研究范畴和研究方法。

> "这种保存有利个体差异及变异、淘汰不利者的现象，
> 我称之为自然选择，或者适者生存。"
>
> —— 查尔斯·达尔文：《物种起源》

学科概览

至少早在古希腊时期，学者们就一直在分析自己的心理状态。古希腊哲学家柏拉图*认为，每个不完美的身体里都有一个理性的灵魂，即一个了解完全理性存在的灵魂。据柏拉图称，桌子等实物的存在，无法完全反映自然界之外存在的桌子的基本形式。但之后的哲学家，如柏拉图的学生亚里士多德*，反倒认为人们可以通过调查足够多的桌子，来进行理性推理以确定何为"桌子"。[2]

一千年后的欧洲文艺复兴时期，法国哲学家勒内·笛卡尔等也试图精确描述心理的定义。笛卡尔宣称，只有人类才拥有思想，它是我们自身无形的一面，"提供了意识、自由选择和理性。"[3]笛卡尔用最著名的一句话"我思故我在"描述了这个过程。他肯定自己是存在的，至少心理是存在的，因为他有心理活动。由此，笛卡尔得出结论，无形的心理控制着有形的肉体（这就是"二元论"，即人类是由心理和身体构成的）。在理性思维的驱动下，人类是先天具有思维的肉食动物。

经验主义者，比如17世纪的英国哲学家约翰·洛克*，就提出了相反的观点。洛克将人心比作一张白纸，当我们在现实世界中感知事物时，它就会被涂上颜色。一切都是物质的，思想只是反映了我们大脑的感官体验。18世纪的苏格兰哲学家大卫·休谟认为，行为源于感情（即情感），人类的行为在很大程度上具有确定性，

也符合自然规则。人类的行为都具有恒常而普遍的规则。人类只是对外界环境有感知，并做出机械的反应：思想是被动的，它随着周围环境的变动而改变。

学术渊源

前文列出的思想家或多或少都被称为哲学家。詹姆斯深受哲学影响，也被心理学和自然科学所吸引。在德国，詹姆斯在医生威廉·冯特和赫尔曼·冯·亥姆霍兹手下做研究的经历使他对心理学产生了浓厚的兴趣。

英国博物学家查尔斯·达尔文也对詹姆斯产生了同样强大的影响。达尔文提出了自然选择的进化理论，这一理论本质上主张，那些适应环境的个体更有可能生存和繁殖，并把特性传给下一代。詹姆斯认为，达尔文推断的生物在某些方面具有"适应性"的观点，可被应用于生物的行为和特征分析。他引入了一个叫作"机能主义"*的概念，将达尔文的原则扩展到心理的研究中。机能特征可以提高生物体的繁殖能力——这是自然选择的基本原则。因为人类是进化的产物，人类的行为和心理状态与生理习性有着某种联系，且一定是由于适应环境的需要而形成的。这并不是说詹姆斯是纯粹的唯物主义者*，而是说，在他看来，生物体在适应环境的过程中，其意识具有机能性。[4]

---

1. B. R. 赫根汉：《心理学史导论》，贝尔蒙特：沃兹沃斯出版社，2009 年，第 2 页。
2. 赫根汉：《心理学史导论》，第 49—50 页。

3. 赫根汉：《心理学史导论》，第 121 页。

4. 詹姆斯受达尔文影响的更多信息，请参阅罗伯特·J. 理查兹："科学中的个人等式：威廉·詹姆斯对达尔文理论的心理和道德运用"，马克·R. 施韦恩编，《威廉·詹姆斯的文艺复兴：青年学者的四篇随笔》，《哈佛图书馆公报》第 30 卷，1982 年第 4 期，第 387—425 页。

3 主导命题

要点 ⚷

- 在詹姆斯的时代，虽然大多数人都觉得心理学具有魅力，但还没有人把它确立为一门科学。

- 基于前辈心理学家和哲学家提出的观点与假设，詹姆斯又提出了一系列新颖的概念。

- 詹姆斯根据基本心理学问题提出了新问题，比如"什么是经验？"和"内省法，即研究自身的心理过程，是否能洞察心灵及其生理轨迹？"

核心问题

威廉·詹姆斯的《心理学原理》提出了这样的问题，人们如何能够发现并系统地阐述心理学科的基本定义？詹姆斯探索了心理的本质，并探究了是否可以将心理理解为"真实的"和有目的的事物这一问题。他还探寻了意识和思维的本质。这些问题的答案将心理学与其他学科区分开来，例如，化学研究物质，生物学研究生物体，心理学则是研究心理状态。

《心理学原理》重新定义了身体和心理的关系。通过詹姆斯首创的"内省"概念，即"把自己的心理活动整理成报告的形式，然后通过分析报告资料得出某种心理学结论"，[1]《心理学原理》打破了以往的研究风格。这种自我反省的研究方法在"大脑的功能"和"大脑活动的一般条件"等章节中表现得尤为明显。詹姆斯用内省法细致入微地分析了个体的生理和心理状态，这也是《心理学原理》的核心所在。但是，最精准的心理学研究方法还有待确定。因此，《心理学原理》必然要面对一个难以捉摸的研究对象，即便是詹姆斯能干的同行们也无法确定心理学的确切性质。

詹姆斯并不是第一个为建立一门全新学科而奋斗的人，他用很大篇幅阐明了"自我"的含义，并在其中讨论了18世纪哲学家大卫·休谟和伊曼努尔·康德的思想观点。同时，他也从柏拉图这样的古希腊哲学家的思想中寻找灵感。这些先辈们为詹姆斯的新心理学学科以及他那本影响深远的作品奠定了基础。《心理学原理》促进了心理学新领域的发展，增强了这门学科作为一门新的现代科学的合理性。

> "最好将意识状态的描述和解释当作心理学的定义。意识状态指感觉、愿望、情绪、认知、推理、决策、意志等诸如此类。当然，对这些意识状态的'解释'必须在可能的范围内，包括对它们的成因、条件和直接后果的研究。"
>
> ——威廉·詹姆斯：《心理学原理》

参与者

许多人认为德国医生、生理学家、哲学家威廉·冯特是心理学的创始人之一。和詹姆斯一样，冯特也试图把心理学创立为不同于生物学和哲学的一门科学。他在莱比锡大学建立了世界上第一个心理学实验室，是实验心理学流派的代表人物。他相信我们可以通过实验分析，即将意识分解成各元素，以达到理解的目的。在冯特看来，将意识分解成基本元素（反应、感觉等等）可以使我们理解其活动轨迹，詹姆斯则反对这种观点。考虑体系中各组成部分以及各部分结合成的整体，这种方法被称为"结构主义"*。

詹姆斯反对的另一种观点是"副现象说"*，即"大脑会导致心理事件，但心理事件不会引发行为。"[2] 这一点至关重要，因为它完全物化了对精神状态的理解：意识是无关紧要的，因为它不会造成任何影响。现象学家把意识比作蒸汽火车上的汽笛。汽笛在火车离开前鸣响，但汽笛对火车的运行没有影响。英国哲学家沙德沃思·霍尔韦·霍奇森*是这一观点的主要支持者。

当时的论战

詹姆斯和他的同时代人争论什么是意识，以及我们应该如何理解意识。《心理学原理》一书中，詹姆斯直接回应了冯特的理论和霍奇森的副现象说。他反对副现象说，认为它的观念无法得到证明，也不切实际。他指出，"副现象学家只是把自动机理论强加给了我们，"并没有提出实证的论点。事实上，他们所做的论证与常识背道而驰，毫无意义，是"在当前的心理学状态下的无理取闹"。[3]

詹姆斯称结构主义为"用实验方法进行的显微式的心理学"。[4] 他认为，结构主义使用的是内省法，但经过了统计法的处理。从根本上来说，詹姆斯认为结构主义提出了错误的问题。"结构主义专注于研究精神生活的各个元素，并根据其中内含的（更优化的）结果去剖析这些元素，"他写道，并将它们简化为"数量尺度"。[5] 因此，詹姆斯认为不应用这种方法研究人的意识，他表示，意识并不适合比较和量化。

1. 威廉·詹姆斯：《心理学原理》（第1—2卷），马萨诸塞州坎布里奇：哈佛大学出版社，1981年，第185页。

2. B. R. 赫根汉：《心理学史导论》，贝尔蒙特：沃兹沃斯出版社，2009年，第18页。

3. 詹姆斯：《心理学原理》，第141页。

4. 詹姆斯：《心理学原理》，第192—193页。

5. 詹姆斯：《心理学原理》，第192—193页。

4 作者贡献

要点 🔑

- 在《心理学原理》中，詹姆斯的主要目的是促使人们接受心理学是一门科学。
- 作者对心理学科学本质的讨论引发了对经验的重新分析。
- 《心理学原理》是建立在前辈哲学家和心理学家的研究成果，以及詹姆斯自己的前期研究成果之上的。

作者目标

在《心理学原理》一书中，威廉·詹姆斯开始挖掘一系列概念的科学性，如意识流（共同构成意识心智的回忆、观察和反思的流动）、自我意识（即对自身意识的察觉）、情绪和意志。他对这些概念的分析，有助于将心理学确立为一门正式的科学。这部作品向人们表明心理学可以揭示独特而又重要的心理现象。由此，詹姆斯确立了自己作为美国心理学分支的奠基人地位，他比以往任何一个心理学者都更深入更实际地探索心理体验。

几个世纪以来，哲学家们一直在争论身体和心灵的本质。詹姆斯的作品将这个古老的讨论延伸到了新的心理学领域。然而，他认为，从传统哲学的视角来看，"我们只有提升思考能力，才能意识到内心世界的存在。"[1]

早在1890年《心理学原理》出版之前，詹姆斯就曾向他的编辑承认，这部著作并没有提出一个清晰、系统的观点，来说明心理学现在是什么，也没有回答它应该成为什么。尽管如此，学者们还是认可了它的原创性和价值。作为詹姆斯最伟大的作品，该书在出版一个多世纪后的今天仍然具有非凡的意义，书中的深刻见解也为现代社会个体内心的迷茫做出了解答。即使工业化＊，即令我们逐渐远离农耕社会和农耕经济的过程，加速了人类与自然和社会的疏远，心理学知识也能给予我们每个人应对自己处境的能力。

> "因为人类最先接触的能被感知的是儿童世界的元素，而这些元素将伴随其一生。"
>
> —— 威廉·詹姆斯：《心理学原理》

研究方法

《心理学原理》是建立在古代和近代哲学，以及詹姆斯同时代人在心理学领域所做的贡献的基础之上的。然而，《心理学原理》打破了传统的研究方法，通过内省法来了解个人经验。

就经验的意义而言，内省是对我们自身经验（声音、图像、印象）的一种审视。詹姆斯引导我们将思想的深层含义以及我们表达思想时使用的语言当作心理数据，例如，他认为，"被遗忘之词的韵律可能就在那里，无声无息，等待着被表达出来……每个人都必然知道一些被遗忘诗节中空白韵律的撩人效果，它不安地在人的心中跳动，努力用词句来将自己填补。"[2]

虽然詹姆斯的研究方法可能显得非常个性化和哲学化，但他终究还是一名实用主义者（实用主义是一个流派，其观点是，"任何信念、思想或行为都必须由其后果来评判"）。[3] 换句话说，一个想法是否有效，判断的标准仍然是它的有用程度。对于实用主义者来说，检验可能的真理，标准只有一个：什么能最好地引领我们，什

么能最好地适应生活的方方面面，什么能毫无遗漏地与经验需求的总和相结合。⁴

詹姆斯的实用主义致使他拒绝"灵魂"这一精神概念。在他看来，一个人不能"从灵魂的已知属性中推断出精神生活的任何属性"。如果一个人想要了解世界或者享受自由，他就必须在精神生活中找到"各种现成的角色，并（把它们刻进）灵魂"。⁵ 当我们能够识别不需要永恒灵魂的精神状态，如快乐或饥饿，那么认为灵魂存在并对其进行分析，又能得到什么呢？

时代贡献

詹姆斯的《心理学原理》为心理学成为一门集哲学和生物学概念于一身的正统科学奠定了基础，贡献巨大。当然，詹姆斯的这部恢宏巨作并非凭空出现。一些哲学家、生物学家的著作以及其他对心理学研究有兴趣的学者都或多或少地对詹姆斯的见解产生了影响。其中，查尔斯·达尔文提出的生物进化论对詹姆斯的机能主义——我们的心理进程具有与我们的进化史相关的特定功能的原则——贡献最大。同时，与德国医生威廉·冯特和赫尔曼·冯·亥姆霍兹一起研究的经历也激发了詹姆斯对心理学的兴趣。

在出版前的几年，《心理学原理》中的一些概念在詹姆斯的其他作品中便有迹可循。如，1878 年，詹姆斯讨论了心理状态与外界刺激之间的关系。他指出，"与外部世界的纯粹联系，是一种完全不可能以心理活动的定义为基础的概念。"⁶詹姆斯认为心理状态是人的内部世界，它们作用于外部世界；它们不能仅仅被理解为对外界刺激的反应。从内向外看世界，而不是从外往里看世界，这被称为"先天论"*；此观点源于詹姆斯早期的作品。

1. 威廉·詹姆斯:《心理学原理》(第1—2卷),马萨诸塞州坎布里奇:哈佛大学出版社,1981年,第679页。

2. 詹姆斯:《心理学原理》,第244页。

3. B.R.赫根汉:《心理学史导论》,贝尔蒙特:沃兹沃斯出版社,2009年,第346页。

4. 威廉·詹姆斯:《实用主义》,纽约:多佛出版社,1907年,第39页。

5. 詹姆斯:《心理学原理》,第328—329页。

6. 威廉·詹姆斯:"以通信形式评价斯宾塞对心理的定义",《思辨哲学杂志》第12卷,1878年第1期,第13页。

第二部分：学术思想

5 思想主脉

要点 🔑

- 《心理学原理》探究了思想、情感是如何与大脑联系在一起的。
- 詹姆斯首创了"意识流"的概念，以反映思维在心理中独立运动的方式。
- 詹姆斯认为，我们应将心理学当作一门现代科学加以发展，并促进其向公认的学术学科转变。

核心主题

詹姆斯的《心理学原理》提供了一种心理学的视角，它可以揭示一个人心理的奥秘和动态特性。心理存在于内心世界与外在世界之间，人在内心世界里经历着心理状态的变化，而外在世界即物质世界构成了心理状态。詹姆斯认为，"假设心理和感知觉存在，并且是知识的载体，"那么，这些心理和感知觉与大脑中的物质存在是联系在一起的。[1] 但这并不意味着心理仅仅从大脑的运动中产生；"心理状态的产生依赖于外部环境，同时又作用于环境。"[2]

并不是说，"身体"是一回事，"心理"又是另一回事。更确切地说，人类可以被理解为两者的综合。从这个角度来看，《心理学原理》涉及了心理状态的内容，以及外部世界与这些心理状态之间的对应关系。

詹姆斯还谈到了感觉和知觉。我们可以将"感觉"定义为我们从外部世界收集感官信息的过程；"知觉"代表我们理解感官信息的方式。换句话说，"你对大猩猩的视觉感觉可能包括大小、颜色、体型，而你对它的知觉还包括对其周围环境的感知，与其他事物的关系，以及对大猩猩的个人经验。"[3]

> "由于意识本身并没有被分割成碎片……用'河'或'流'来形容意识是最自然不过的比喻了。在以后的讨论中，让我们称它为思想流、意识流或主观生活流。"
>
> ——威廉·詹姆斯:《心理学原理》

思想探究

虽然很难找到一个"关键观点"，我们也可准确得出《心理学原理》主要讨论了什么是意识。当胃咕噜叫（外在的）时，头脑（内在的）中是否会产生意识呢？又或者意识纯粹与生俱来——是一种本质的、固有的事物？詹姆斯认为，意识不是从感觉中产生的（看到颜色，感到刺痛），无论感知觉强烈与否。意识是**从思想中产生**的。换句话说，詹姆斯的目的不在于分析感知觉，他认为，感知觉的形成可能是一个完全机械的过程，他想要了解意识本身。

这就引出了詹姆斯著名的"意识流"概念。詹姆斯在谈到意识时说，"当它第一次出现时，'链'或'队列'这样的词并不能描述它。它不是一节一节的；它是流动性的。"[4]詹姆斯认为，思想不是由其他感觉组成的，比如对一个黄色球的认识并不是黄色的颜色、圆形的形状、球的概念和用途等认知的集合。首先，对这个黄色球的认知仍是一个完全个人的行为，它不能被分解成任何元素。这种想法不会凭空发生和消失；它仍是思想不断流动的一部分，或者用詹姆斯的比喻来说，是一种流。

如果所有的思想都在彼此的背景下产生和消失，那么"思想之流是如此的迅猛，以至于它总是在我们能够阻止它之前就已经呈现出结论"。[5] 换句话说，思想并不是一个通过元素分解（即"还原论"*）就可以获取、检验和分析的个体对象。相反，"思想"仍然是一个连续的概念，是水流的一部分，它不断变化，但仍在前进。如果我想到一个黄色的球，然后又想到另一个黄色的球，那它们就不一样了，因为那是两个截然不同的先后产生的思想。

詹姆斯将意识描述为一个"同时发生的可能性剧场"，它有选择地权衡思想，并选择保留最有用的。当涉及个人的思想时，意识可以选择"挑选一些思想，通过加强和抑制注意力来压制其余的思想"。[6] 这有益于我们应对这个需要我们关注的复杂世界。[7]

语言表述

《心理学原理》在语言和表达上非常独特。虽然詹姆斯文笔清晰直率，但有些段落仍然晦涩难懂。许多读者发现，该书缺少一个关键的论点。虽然没有清晰的结构，我们依然可以理解作者的大部分，甚至是更深奥和微妙的观点。至少有一点很明确，詹姆斯旨在阐明这一新的现代科学的基本规律。

詹姆斯在《心理学原理》中提出了如此引人注目的论点，以至于他成功地使心理学成为一门正式的学术学科。尽管他想要描述的是个体思想这一众所周知的，但却一直难以被描述的现象，他的表现仍然卓越。

对于绝大多数学者来说，《心理学原理》仍然是心理学研究领域的基础性著作。毫无疑问，它使心理学成为一门现代科学。当然，这部著作也遭到了批评，[8] 甚至作者本人在1890年的一封信中也对自己的著作进行了批判，[9] 但是，没有任何其他作品能

像它一样，在心理学已经开始流行的美国与欧洲，一出版就获得
支持，广受好评。

---

1. 威廉·詹姆斯：《心理学原理》（第1—2卷），马萨诸塞州坎布里奇：哈佛大学
出版社，1981年，第VI页。

2. 詹姆斯：《心理学原理》，第6页。

3. 杰拉尔德·E.迈尔斯："导论：背景知识"，詹姆斯著：《心理学原理》，马萨诸
塞州坎布里奇：哈佛大学出版社，1981年，第XXII—XXIII页。

4. 詹姆斯：《心理学原理》，第239页。

5. 詹姆斯：《心理学原理》，第244页。

6. 詹姆斯：《心理学原理》，第288页。

7. B.R.赫根汉：《心理学史导论》，贝尔蒙特：沃兹沃斯出版社，2009年，第341页。

8. 可参阅威廉·J.加文：《聚焦威廉·詹姆斯：信仰的意志》，布卢明顿：印第安
纳大学出版社，2013年；迈克尔·斯莱特：《威廉·詹姆斯论道德与信仰》，剑
桥：剑桥大学出版社，2009年；迈克尔·约翰逊和特蕾西·亨利编：《对〈心
理学原理〉的反思：一个世纪后的威廉·詹姆斯》，新泽西州希尔斯代尔：劳伦
斯·艾尔伯协会，1990年；詹姆斯·鲍威斯基：《詹姆斯的动态个人主义》，纽
约州奥尔巴尼：纽约州立大学出版社，2007年；罗素·古德曼："威廉·詹姆
斯"，爱德华·扎尔塔编，《斯坦福哲学百科全书》，2013年，登录日期2016年2
月9日，http://plato.stanford.edu/entries/james/。

9. 亨利·詹姆斯编：《威廉·詹姆斯的书信》，波士顿：利特尔＆布朗出版社，
1926年，第393—394页。

6 思想支脉

要点 🗝

- 《心理学原理》探讨的是我们如何从心理学的视角去理解感知觉。
- 因为詹姆斯只关注我们是如何看和如何听的，所以他的分析是支离破碎的。
- 仔细观察，不难发现詹姆斯对个人心理的一些不经意的观察有着深层的含义。

其他思想

除了"意识流"的概念，威廉·詹姆斯的《心理学原理》还探究了许多其他关键论题。我们应注意，詹姆斯或许并不认同人们把"意识流"称为他的主要心理学思想。因为，除了"意识流"之外，他提出的其他新观点也是非常值得探讨的。

首先，詹姆斯讨论了习惯、本能，以及人们的行为是经过选择的结果还是仅仅凭直觉行事这一问题。一位学者曾指出，"詹姆斯并不认为人类的本能行为是盲目和不可改变的"，而是我们意识到的行为，"可通过经验而改变"。[1] 换句话说，大多数人喜欢睡在柔软的床垫上而不喜欢睡在坚硬的地板上，喜欢吃牛排而不是泥土。自身的经验让他们宁愿选择舒适生活而不选择节俭度日。相反，想想一些无意识的行为，比如，当我站在一个房间里时，我总是面对着房间中心位置，因为我以前这样做过很多次，我的大脑已经习惯了这种活动。[2] 内部和外部的因素在这里仍然很重要：根据外部因素，当我们进入一个房间时，我们会自动地面对房间的中心（而不是墙壁）。根据内部因素，我们可以通过每次进入房间时面对墙壁来改变这种行为，以产生其他的外部暗示。我们并非生来就有这些偏好（床、牛排、面对房间的中心）。它们代表了通过训练形成的行为模式。这种训练在大脑中创造了一条神经通路，简单说就是改变了我们大脑的结构。

詹姆斯探讨情绪的方式如出一辙。他认为情绪不只是外部事物引起的精神震荡，而是由外部刺激和身体反应相互作用的结果。情绪不只是作为一种精神状态存在，它是一种生理状态：愤怒让我们脸红心跳加速，肌肉紧张。因此，当我看到一只熊并感到害怕，事实上这只熊本身并不会制造这种恐惧，而是看到熊会引起我的生理反应，这种反应让我感到害怕。[3]

> "那么，在所有的教育中，最重要的是让我们的神经系统成为我们的盟友而不是敌人。它为我们的将来提供资金和资本，使我们获得收益从而过上轻松生活。为此，我们必须尽可能早地采取自发的、习以为常的、有用的行动，并防止其发展成为可能对我们不利的方式，正如我们应该预防瘟疫一样。"
>
> ——威廉·詹姆斯：《心理学原理》

思想探究

在詹姆斯看来，我们通过外部和内部因素调节习惯和情绪，自由意志*在这一过程中起着重要作用。我们的意识和回忆是选择性的和个性化的：我们选择想要经历的人生，选择理解我们所经历事件的方式。詹姆斯认为，习惯"注定了我们所有人都要根据自己的教育环境或早期的选择来面对各自的人生，并尽最大努力去追求不适宜自己的人生，因为我们已别无选择，现在重新开始又为时已晚"。[4]

但习惯并不一定决定命运，意志可以培养习惯改变习惯。如果你从小就吃健康的食物，你会养成健康饮食的习惯；[5] 如果你从小就吃不健康的食物，成年之后你也会养成健康饮食的习惯。所以，一个人的行为是意识和身体共同作用的结果。

一个人的情绪源于类似的相互作用，并且同样服从于意识。詹姆斯曾说："吹口哨壮胆绝不只是一种修辞手段。"[6] 一个人情绪的变化源于身体的感知，内在状态的改变源于外部状态的改变（心理状态变为生理状态）。但是人可以决定自己应有的心理状态，并且努力改变现实环境——吹口哨而不是畏畏缩缩——从而改变心理状态。在詹姆斯之后，丹麦医生卡尔·兰格* 提出了相似的理论。这一观点被称为"詹姆斯—兰格"情绪理论。

无论是行为还是情绪，我们所分配的注意力都会不同。詹姆斯认为"注意力是意志的基本现象"。[7] 大多数时候，人类仍然是习性动物，其受保护的神经通路会不断受到外界事件的冲击。但是通过意识的选择和注意力的提升，我们可以实现一些接近自由意志的东西。

被忽视之处

在《心理学原理》的所有观点中，威廉·詹姆斯对感知觉过程的讨论可能受到了一些轻微的忽视。事实上，这一领域的研究人员，在很大程度上忽略了詹姆斯对相关研究领域的贡献，正如一位评论人士所言，"对于感觉和感知的话题，作家和研究人员很少引用詹姆斯的观点甚至术语作为自己作品的理论依据，甚至是对他们自己作品的影响也很少提及，这与人们对待他提出的依然盛行的情绪观点形成了鲜明的对比。"[8] 尽管，詹姆斯关于感知觉的章节"都来自'真实生活'和实验的深刻见解和实例"。詹姆斯的感知觉理论"至少能够……帮助学生和研究人员锁定细微问题"，即能"在一个更丰富、更广泛的心理／哲学语境下"分析细微的问题。[9]

为什么学者们大都忽略了詹姆斯的感知觉观点呢？是因为詹姆斯没有用足够的篇章来论述吗？[10] 相反，詹姆斯实际上"用了许多篇章来讨论感知觉问题"。但一些人还是认为，"在詹姆斯对待感觉和知觉的方式上，我们只能看到表面的东西，而不是智慧的和见多识广的观点。"[11]

1. B. R. 赫根汉：《心理学史导论》，贝尔蒙特：沃兹沃斯出版社，2009 年，第 342 页。
2. 赫根汉：《心理学史导论》，第 342 页。
3. 赫根汉：《心理学史导论》，第 344 页。
4. 威廉·詹姆斯：《心理学原理》（第 1—2 卷），马萨诸塞州坎布里奇：哈佛大学出版社，1981 年，第 121 页。
5. 詹姆斯：《心理学原理》，第 11 页。
6. 詹姆斯：《心理学原理》，第 576 页。
7. 詹姆斯：《心理学原理》，第 317 页。
8. 威廉·N. 登伯：《威廉·詹姆斯的感觉与知觉》，《心理科学》第 1 卷，1990 年第 3 期，第 163—166 页。
9. 登伯：《威廉·詹姆斯的感觉与知觉》，第 166 页。
10. 登伯：《威廉·詹姆斯的感觉与知觉》，第 164 页。
11. 登伯：《威廉·詹姆斯的感觉与知觉》，第 166 页。

7 历史成就

要点 ⚿—

- 《心理学原理》促进创立了一门新的科学。为此目的，詹姆斯分析了从古代哲学到宗教的主题。

- 詹姆斯《心理学原理》之后的作品和演讲，特别是《宗教经验种种》和《信仰的意志》，都进一步拓展了《心理学原理》中的思维模式。

- 随着认知科学* 在 20 世纪 60 年代的诞生（关于心理处理信息的方式的科学），学者们很快就放弃了詹姆斯的一些观点，他们再一次将目光聚焦于人类思想的内部运作过程，然而，早在七十多年前詹姆斯就曾研究过这一领域。

观点评价

在《心理学原理》中，威廉·詹姆斯主要揭示的是心理学的基本定律。詹姆斯以一种独特的方式——内省法，分析了他的观察结果，展示了心理学的本质和力量。这一点在作品中对个人经验的探索方面尤为明显。

在许多方面，詹姆斯并不欣然接受外界对自己的高度赞誉。一位评论员曾写道，"19 世纪 70 年代，詹姆斯在哈佛大学建立了第一个心理学实验室，给美国带来了新的学科实验心理学。"但他"对这种评价从来都没有什么热情，总是与其保持着距离"。[1] 现代心理学流派因詹姆斯促进心理学成为一门科学的贡献将其称为先驱者，但如果詹姆斯还活着，他可能并不完全认同此殊荣。

对于一个学者来说，"今天的心理学就是詹姆斯所概述的那种心理学"，因为它"愿意运用有效的方法去探究人类存在的所有方面"。[2] 这可能是一个很精辟的论点，但这并不出自詹姆斯之口。詹姆斯这样评论自己的著作："没有什么问题值得一千页来论述。"他觉得自己只研究了皮毛并不专注，为此他总结道，"第一，没有所谓的心理科学；第二，（威廉·詹姆斯）是个无能之辈。"[3]

> "威廉·詹姆斯是一位对生理学、心理学和哲学及其交叉学科有独到见解的思想家。他长达一千二百页的杰作《心理学原理》是一本集生理学、心理学、哲学和个人思考于一身的丰富著作，它给了我们诸如'思想之流'和婴儿眼中的世界'极度模糊、嗡嗡作响、一片混乱'（第 462 页）这样的想法。它包含实用主义和现象学的种子，影响了欧洲和美国的几代思想家，包括埃德蒙德·胡塞尔 *、伯特兰·罗素、约翰·杜威、路德维希·维特根斯坦。"
>
> ——罗素·古德曼 *："威廉·詹姆斯"，《斯坦福哲学百科全书》

当时的成就

品读詹姆斯的其他作品会使读者对《心理学原理》有更为深刻的理解。另外两部使他声名鹊起的作品是《宗教经验种种》和《信仰的意志》。在这两本书中，詹姆斯对宗教经验的讨论都有所扩展，从他最早的散文开始，一直到《心理学原理》，都有涉及这个主题。

尽管詹姆斯之前的作品使他广为人知，但他的《心理学原理》得到了国际社会的一致认可。然而，他却曾公开声称自己对这部作品的篇幅感到厌恶。确实，《心理学原理》的篇幅长达两卷。詹姆斯在 1892 年修订了该书并出版了单卷本《心理学简编》。[4] "《心理学原理》几乎一半的内容都被重写或被增加新内容。多年来,《心理学简编》一直是最受欢迎的心理学英语读物,因其简短精悍,通常被称作'吉米读物'"。[5]

但是,无论是詹姆斯所推崇的内省法,还是《心理学原理》和《心理学简编》中个人对心理过程的反思,都很快失宠。学者们用更多分析性的、以实验为基础的方法取代了它们。"詹姆斯贬低它们为'实验室里的无赖'(贬义),正把心理学带向他不愿追随的方向。"之后,詹姆斯逐渐放弃心理学,转向哲学研究。[6]

局限性

《心理学原理》对心理学作为一门科学的确立产生了深刻的影响。但詹姆斯的某些观点仍有一定的局限性。詹姆斯支持机能主义,一个主要研究行为和意识的功能**目的**的流派。[7]他提供了一个新的视角,与德国心理学家、哲学家威廉·冯特和英国心理学家爱德华·铁钦纳倡导的结构主义截然对立(结构主义指分析构成系统的各个元素的方法)。一些学者跳出来批判詹姆斯,包括他的老师威廉·冯特,一位学者写道,"经验主义者冯特在读了詹姆斯的《心理学原理》后,评价其为'一部出色的文学作品,但不是心理学著作'"。[8]"经验主义"*指以实验为核心的心理学方法。虽然机能主义对美国心理学有着重要影响,但机能主义"不科学"的研究角度,整体上削弱了它在心理学上的地位。

评论家还指出,詹姆斯的内省法在本质上仍然是纯主观的。心理学家很快开始探索更客观的方法来研究心理和行为。事实上,到了20世纪20年代,行为主义*,一种通过行为分析来确定心理过程的可观察的方法,已经开始比詹姆斯的机能主义更加突出。詹姆斯关于心智的许多观点被（显性的）可见的行为取代。

有些行为主义者对"行为只可以被描述和解释，而不涉及心理事件或心理过程"这一观点很是赞同。[9] 但是，随着 20 世纪 60 年代认知科学的诞生，新一代的研究人员试图以系统的、可靠的方式了解心理和认知过程，技术的进步使得他们能够做到这一点。

1. 爱德华·S.里德：《从灵魂到心理：心理学的产生（从伊拉斯谟斯·达尔文到威廉·詹姆斯）》，康涅狄格州纽黑文：耶鲁大学出版社，1997 年，第 201 页。

2. B. R. 赫根汉：《心理学史导论》，贝尔蒙特：沃兹沃斯出版社，2009 年，第 377 页。

3. 威廉·詹姆斯：《心理学原理》（第 1—2 卷），马萨诸塞州坎布里奇：哈佛大学出版社，1981 年，第 294 页。

4. 威廉·詹姆斯：《心理学简编》，马萨诸塞州坎布里奇和伦敦：哈佛大学出版社，1984 年。

5. 杰拉尔德·E.迈尔斯："导论：背景知识"，《心理学原理》，第 XXXVI 页。

6. 兰德·B.埃文斯："导论：历史背景"，《心理学原理》，第 XI 页。

7. 坎德拉·彻丽："结构主义和功能主义：心理学早期思想流派"，About.com，登录日期 2016 年 1 月 17 日，http://psychology.about.com/od/historyofpsychology/a/structuralism.htm。

8. B. R. 赫根汉和特蕾西·B.亨利：《心理学史导论》，贝尔蒙特：沃兹沃斯出版社，2013 年，第 326 页。

9. 乔治·格雷瓦姆，"行为主义"，《斯坦福哲学百科全书》，登录日期 2016 年 1 月 17 日，http://plato.stanford.edu/archives/sum2012/entries/behaviorism/。

8 著作地位

要点 🔑

- 在整个作品中，詹姆斯主要关注是人的心理状态，生理体征以及体表信号。

- 詹姆斯的作品并没有统一的主题，都引用了日常生活中的实例来阐释他的理论。

- 尽管詹姆斯不是第一次，也不是最后一次取得这样的成就，《心理学原理》仍然是他的遗产基石，并巩固了他作为"心理学之父"的美誉。

定位

1890 年《心理学原理》出版时，威廉·詹姆斯已成为心理学的主要支持者和一门科学的创始人。早在 1878 年，他就对心理学产生了浓厚的兴趣，当时他发表了一篇名为《以通信形式评价斯宾塞对心理的定义》的文章。[1]第二年，他又发表了另一篇文章《理性情感》(再版于《信仰的意志和通俗哲学论文集》)，[2]并于 1882 年进行了修订并再版。某种意义上，这两篇著作都以多种方式预示了《心理学原理》的问世。

《心理学原理》之后，詹姆斯的作品都或多或少地与它有着明确的联系。比如 1897 年的初版《信仰的意志》、出版于 1902 年的《宗教经验种种》，[3]以及詹姆斯的晚年作品：1907 年的《实用主义》、[4]1909 年的《多元的宇宙》、[5]1912 年的《彻底的经验主义》。[6]

在詹姆斯的著作中，我们不难发现他一直在积极地探索和思考，但探索的核心，即他毕生对心理学基本定律的探索，并没有出现在他所有的作品中。我们不妨把《心理学原理》当作一面棱镜来观察他早期和后期的作品，遗憾的是，包括《心理学原理》在内的很多作品，都缺乏清晰的中心思想。这使得学者们面临巨大挑战，他们试图将詹姆斯的主要作品整理成一个连贯的体系。一些学者指出，詹姆斯的作品仍然具有独特的重要性，因为它们为不确定性提供了极为深刻的阐释。

> 威廉·詹姆斯的思想概括了哲学和心理学之间的矛盾关系。
>
> ——杰拉尔德·E. 迈尔斯："导论"，威廉·詹姆斯著，
> 《心理学原理》

整合

詹姆斯的主要作品并不是连贯统一的，尽管他的每一部作品都有明显的主题。有些是偶然的，比如詹姆斯反驳威廉·冯特关于每一个故意行为都包含一个独特的感觉的观点，他提出了"感觉神经支配 *"的含义。

在《心理学原理》和其他作品中，詹姆斯用日常生活的事例（不系统，甚至，看起来还有些琐碎）来论证他的理论观点："晚饭后我坐在桌子旁，时不时地从盘子里拿坚果或葡萄干吃。我的晚餐结束了，在激烈的谈话中我几乎意识不到我在做什么；但是，对这种水果的感知，以及我可能会吃它的转瞬即逝的想法，似乎促成了这一行为。这里当然没有明确的指令（即命令或要求）。"[7]

意义

学者往往将詹姆斯称为"美国心理学之父"，把他的非凡成就和其他科学领域的元勋如让-马丁·沙可*（神经学*领域的先驱，神经学即大脑和神经系统的科学）和西格蒙德·弗洛伊德*（精神分析法*的创始人，精神分析法即潜意识的治疗方法和理论研究方法）等比肩。像他们一样，詹姆斯为使他的学科成为一门现代科学提供了强有力的论证。《心理学原理》从内在和外在两个视角去解析心理现象，见解独特。此外，詹姆斯对经验的探索增强了我们对洞察力的理解，他恰好转变了我们对如何获得经验的思考。

詹姆斯的创新为心理学提供了全新的机会，使人们了解了非心理活动。心理学家们——事实上，还有科学领域以外的人，包括艺术家们——不再把心理当作一系列静态的图像来分析，而是把经验看作是不断流动的意识流。

作为一名哲学家，威廉·詹姆斯享有权威人物的地位。一位评论员写道："威廉·詹姆斯对美国古典哲学的贡献，就如柏拉图对希腊和罗马哲学的贡献一样。"[8]詹姆斯的作品在心理学领域至关重要，例如意识流或思维本身是一种活动的概念。他的实用主义方法也重新定义了这门学科。实用主义仍然是美国哲学独特的研究方法。詹姆斯提出了与欧洲同行不同的观点，即根据实际价值提出了类似"灵魂存在吗？"这样的问题：答案是否以最简单可行的方式告诉我们一些现实又独特的东西呢？由于这些原因，詹姆斯的主要作品，尤其是《心理学原理》一直广受好评。

1. 威廉·詹姆斯："以通信形式评价斯宾塞对心理的定义"，《思辨哲学杂志》第 12 卷，1878 年第 1 期，第 1—18 页。

2. 威廉·詹姆斯：《信仰的意志和通俗哲学论文集》，马萨诸塞州坎布里奇和伦敦：哈佛大学出版社，1979 年。

3. 威廉·詹姆斯：《宗教经验种种》，纽约：巴诺书局，2004 年。

4. 威廉·詹姆斯：《实用主义》，纽约：多佛出版社，1907 年。

5. 威廉·詹姆斯：《多元的宇宙》，马萨诸塞州坎布里奇：哈佛大学出版社，1909 年。

6. 威廉·詹姆斯：《彻底的经验主义》，伦敦：朗曼斯·格林公司，1912 年。

7. 威廉·詹姆斯：《心理学原理》（第 1—2 卷），马萨诸塞州坎布里奇：哈佛大学出版社，1981 年，第 1131 页。

8. 约翰·麦克德莫特：引自小理查德·D. 理查森，《传记：处于美国现代主义漩涡中的威廉·詹姆斯》，波士顿：水手出版社，2006 年，第 XIV 页。

第三部分：学术影响

9 最初反响

要点 🔑

- 尽管人们对《心理学原理》褒贬不一，评论家们从来没有一致反对过这部著作。

- 詹姆斯认为同行们对新科学表现出过度的崇拜，这位"心理学之父"便渐渐远离了心理学。

- 詹姆斯为机能主义学派的广为传播奠定了基础；之后的心理学家充实发展了机能主义理论的原理。

批评

威廉·詹姆斯的《心理学原理》受到的评价褒贬不一，这或许是可以理解的，因为它所考察的主题范围之广却没有一个中心论题。书中的个别部分如詹姆斯提出的"意识流"概念得到了普遍赞扬，而内省法则引起争论——自省被指责不是客观（公平、公正）的分析，是最不利心理学研究的方法。例如，哲学家 C. S. 皮尔斯 * 写道，詹姆斯的内省方法等同于"对数据的不加鉴别的接受……这将与公认的心理学和一般科学研究方法彻底决裂"。[1]

总的来说，评论家们认为，纵然《心理学原理》见解深刻、理论出色、意义深远、哲学性强，但它与日益流行的、把心理学当作生物学那样的"硬"科学的趋势相冲突。西班牙哲学家乔治·桑塔亚纳 *，一直对詹姆斯将物质原因归咎于心理影响的观点持怀疑态度。引用那些认为所有现象应由生理原因解释的"唯物主义者"的观点，他写道，詹姆斯已经超越唯物主义者本身，将"心灵完全而直接依赖于物质领域的原则应用于多个领域，而我们仍然只习惯形而上学 * 或心理学的假设"[2]（"形而上学"指的是哲学的分支，研究最基本问题，即存在论和知识论）。

> "幸运的是，对威廉·詹姆斯来说，关于美国心理学、哲学和一般的美国文学，他对自身、对自己的著作及其未来的估计都大错特错。对美国心理学来说，詹姆斯的《心理学原理》是传统哲学心理学和新的实验心理学之间的分界点。"
>
> —— 兰德·B. 埃文斯："历史背景"，威廉·詹姆斯著，《心理学原理》

回应

在回应一位评论家时，詹姆斯使用了一些强有力的语言为自己辩护。他说，他之所以选择不系统地写作，是因为"对那些在心理学文献中占主导地位的专业术语和状态描述充满了强烈的厌恶感。"[3]最终，同行们的科学幻想使得詹姆斯逐渐放弃了实验心理学。他发现，这门学科渐渐变成他所认为的"吹毛求疵"的物理科学，经验积累得越来越多，却没有思考和新的发明。虽然，1892 年他重新出版了该书的简本，即众所周知的"吉米"版。[4]但其核心思想并没有改变，即身体与心灵之间的关系，以及"意识流"概念。

他在最后一部心理学作品《情感的生理基础》[5]中，更加全面地回应了评论家们的言论。书中，他重申了这样一种情况，即快乐和痛苦之类的简单感觉不是由特殊神经传播的（正如还原论者所说的那样），而是因精神状态和生理刺激的相互作用而产生的。

冲突与共识

詹姆斯为后来的机能心理学定下了基调（根据这一理论，在进化史的要求下，精神状态必须具有某种功能）。但直到 20 世纪，有影响力的心理学家约翰·杜威和詹姆斯·安吉尔*"强调了适应性行为的功能意义，并将思维视为环境与机体需求之间的媒介，"[6] 机能主义学派才盛行起来。这种思维方式超越了内省法。因为这些新的机能主义者只研究可以观察到的事物。

许多早期行为学家（对他们来说，心理研究只能通过所观察事物来进行，如行为）开始了他们作为机能主义者的学术生涯。一位学者指出，有些人"对在不借助内省法的情况下，能够了解到的人类知识的广度印象深刻，于是他们开始倾向于后来被称为行为主义的流派"。[7] 机能主义心理学家詹姆斯·卡特尔*写道，"心理过程的持续时间，感知和运动的准确性，意识的范围，疲劳和练习，伴随思想活动的记忆与联系，空间的感知"能够用纯实验的、可观察的方法进行分析。"我调查过（这些现象），在实验过程中，不需要对研究对象进行任何反省，也不需要对自己进行反省。"[8] 换句话说，卡特尔认为内省是不科学的，也认为把心理学作为一门科学是不值得的。

---

1. C. S. 皮尔斯:《皮尔斯著作集》(第 8 卷: 1890—1892)，皮尔斯版项目，2010 年，第 234 页。

2. 乔治·桑塔亚纳：引自杰拉尔德·E.迈尔斯，"导论：背景知识"，《心理学原理》（第1—2卷），马萨诸塞州坎布里奇：哈佛大学出版社，1981年，第XXXVII—XXXVIII 页。

3. 迈克尔·M.索卡尔："威廉·詹姆斯简介"，《心理学简编》，马萨诸塞州坎布里奇和伦敦：哈佛大学出版社，1984年，第 XXXVIII 页。

4. 威廉·詹姆斯：《心理学简编》。

5. 威廉·詹姆斯："情感的生理基础"，《心理评论》第101卷，1994年第2期，第205—210页。

6. O. L. 赞格威尔：《牛津大学的同伴的想法》，理查德·L.格雷戈里编，登录日期 2016 年 2 月 8 日，http://ezproxy-prd.bodleian.ox.ac.uk:2232/view/10.1093/acref/9780198662242.001.0001/acref-9780198662242-e-356?rskey=xS72i4&result=1。

7. B. R. 赫根汉：《心理学史导论》，贝尔蒙特：沃兹沃斯出版社，2009年，第384页。

8. 赫根汉：《心理学史导论》，第384页。

10 后续争议

要点 🗝—

- 詹姆斯的作品吸引了众多追随者，现象学（探讨感知觉和知识习得的问题）和格式塔心理学*（该思想流派将心理和生理视为一个整体，而并非两个单独的组成部分）领域都深受詹姆斯启发。

- 虽然詹姆斯的观点从未形成一个思想流派，但他的见解仍然鼓舞人心。

- 不少现代思想家都从詹姆斯的作品中受益，比如 20 世纪的奥地利裔英国语言哲学家路德维希·维特根斯坦。

应用与问题

在《心理学原理》中，威廉·詹姆斯提出了一种机能主义的方法，他认为，根据人类进化史，心理现象对人类有机体的某些功能至关重要。这种方法引发了与结构主义学派的争论，对他们来说，心理可以（应该）仅仅被认为是一个由反应和感觉等综合成分组成的系统。两个学派争论不休直到机能主义学说被学界广泛接受。

机能主义与现象学有关，现象学是由心理学家、哲学家埃德蒙德·胡塞尔创立的，胡塞尔是另一位受詹姆斯影响的学者。有些学派仅仅把心理现象看成是要素，现象学则把它们看成是一个整体，但不是部分的总和。

当看到一个苹果时，胡塞尔会对这个苹果的各个方面进行整体描述，而其他思想流派的学者只会进行片面的描述，比如看到苹果的颜色是"红"的，形状是"圆"的，它是水果等特性。而现象学把感知觉视为一种整体体验。我们应先对事物有个整体的感知，而不是问别人是怎么看的。毕竟，我们不是通过几个音符判断出是交响乐，而是通过音乐所激发的整体印象来判断。

格式塔心理学派的心理学家们，被认为是胡塞尔的追随者，他们吸收了詹姆斯的"意识流"概念。他们认为，我们可以根据心理的要素来研究心理，但前提是我们必须清楚，这些要素是由整体思想组成的。"Gestalt"在德语中的意思是"整体"，格式塔心理学由此而来。

格式塔心理学的评论家们，常常听起来很像早期批判詹姆斯作品的那些人。他们称格式塔心理学是不精确且主观的（格式塔学家将其视为一种长处）。最终，这一理论流派被其他的心理学流派吸收了（尤其被主流学派精神分析学、行为主义学和认知科学所替代）。

> "经过一系列的实验，这项工作得以完成。通过这些实验，我们（在很大程度上）学会了在没有'一夫多妻制'和奴隶制、私人战争和杀戮自由、司法酷刑和专制皇权的情况下生活。"
>
> ——罗素·古德曼，威廉·詹姆斯著，《信仰的意志》

思想流派

美国哲学家约翰·杜威开创了机能主义思想流派。杜威认为，心理学的要素是由进化决定的。换句话说，意识帮助人们在复杂的选项之间做出选择。杜威将詹姆斯的"意识流"原理应用于行为，认为行为也是一个"流"。当其他思想家把行为分成不同元素（刺激和反应）进行分析时，杜威却没有。他举了一个儿童和蜡烛的例子，儿童伸手抓握蜡烛的火焰，然后缩回手掌。杜威指出，"被燃烧的经历，改变了儿童对火焰的感知。"[1] 这种情况只有当"儿童看到烛光时，蜡烛仍在燃烧，才会发生，儿童就会缩回手掌了……所谓的刺激和反应不是分离的，而是一个相互联系的机能事件序列，之后儿童再不会受烛光吸引，而是选择回避"。[2]

心理学家 E. L. 桑戴克 * 进一步发展了机能心理学，并将其纳入实验室研究。桑戴克是詹姆斯的学生之一，他提出了练习律与效果律。效果律表明，某种特定刺激可能会产生几种可能的反应，最符合动物意愿的反应最有可能反复出现，而不符合动物意愿的反应最不可能重复出现。练习律指出，若一个可变的联结得到使用，刺激与反应之间的联结就得到加强。[3] 最终，科学家们将机能主义的主要观点纳入更广泛的心理学研究中。这一发展在很大程度上归功于机能主义的语用方法以及行为具有进化功能的假设。

当代研究

20 世纪奥地利裔英国语言哲学家维特根斯坦，是詹姆斯的追随者之一。与詹姆斯关于思想和意识的讨论相比，维特根斯坦对詹姆斯的实用主义更感兴趣。《心理学原理》中称维特根斯坦具有"实用主义哲学人格"；"他理智又时刻保持热情以避免受理论束缚，协调受理论化驱使的人类利益，并且足够灵活，可以带着疑问继续前进"。[4]

维特根斯坦 1953 年的著作《哲学研究》影响力巨大，旨在揭示语言的原理。维特根斯坦认为，语言都受到经验的制约；语言不仅是"词语的集合"，而且具有整体的意义。[5] 就拿"谢谢我的幸运星。"这句话来说，如果一个古罗马人这样说，它表达了对他所信仰的对自己起作用的某个神圣实体的真诚感谢。但是，一个现代人也会用同样的语言来表达他的信仰，但这仅是一种比喻说法。

所以，维特根斯坦认为，语言没有普遍的规律，我们也不能把它分解成各个部分去理解。我们必须把语言放在语境中去理解，并且认识到，不同语境中的话语会有不同的含义。当有人站在图书馆里说："看看我的家族树"，他可能指的是他的家谱文件。但如果有人站在田野里说了同样的话，他可能指的是他家族土地上的一棵树。

1. B. R. 赫根汉：《心理学史导论》，贝尔蒙特：沃兹沃斯出版社，2009 年，第 363 页。

2. 赫根汉：《心理学史导论》，第 363 页。

3. 赫根汉：《心理学史导论》，第 342—343 页。

4. 罗素·古德曼：《维特根斯坦与威廉·詹姆斯》，剑桥：剑桥大学出版社，2002 年，第 19 页。

5. 路德维希·维特根斯坦：《哲学研究》，P. M. S. 哈克和乔基姆·舒尔特译，奇切斯特：约翰威立国际出版公司，2009 年。

11 当代印迹

要点 🔑

- 一个多世纪以来，《心理学原理》一直是心理学史上的一部重要著作。

- 行为主义者一直都在借鉴詹姆斯的机能主义思想，直到今天仍然如此。

- 现今，科学家致力于研究人工智能的问题；认知心理学家通过讨论"意识"的定义以及表现意识的人或事扩展了詹姆斯的研究。

地位

威廉·詹姆斯的《心理学原理》仍然是心理学和哲学史上的一部重要著作，即使它不再在现代思想流派中扮演重要角色。对心理学的研究已经从詹姆斯的内省法转向了形式逻辑、神经科学（研究神经系统和大脑的科学）、对照实验。虽然《心理学原理》不再是心理学的教科书，但它仍然是心理学和哲学史上的一部重要作品。[1]

"在 20 世纪，提到《心理学原理》可能只起着装饰门面的作用。（20 世纪下半叶，）在主流实验心理学领域，提及詹姆斯，通常都是对其历史性的贡献赞不绝口，而不是对詹姆斯思想的认真思考。"[2] 然而，美国著名心理学家戈登·奥尔波特*认为，我们可以从《心理学原理》中得到一些基本的经验："狭隘的一致性既不能拯救科学，也无助于人类。让你的方法多样化……即使你发现自己陷入悖论，那又如何？"[3] 换句话说，詹姆斯一直以来都建议心理学家和哲学家应当在研究中讲求实际，如果对自己的研究的有效性无益，就不要过分地局限于一种方法。

> 习惯是社会庞大的制动轮，是社会的最可贵的守恒力，只有习惯能使我们人人安分守己，能使富人免受穷人的妒忌抗议。
>
> —— 威廉·詹姆斯：《心理学原理》

互动

随着詹姆斯与其追随者的关注，行为主义学派不断发展。行为主义者认为，心理学应该关注可观察的行为，而不是心理状态或思想。20 世纪的心理学家 B. F. 斯金纳 * 进一步发展了行为主义，创立了名为"激进行为主义"的学派。斯金纳称"内省"是一个模糊的过程，他相信人们会用诸如"满意""选择"等心理词汇来猜测他们大脑中发生的神经活动。斯金纳写道："一门完全独立的主观经验科学与行为科学的关系，还比不上人们对火的感受与燃烧学的关系。"[4]

与必须解释和报告的精神状态调查不同，行为主义假设科学家只能估量行为和决定行为的外部刺激。正如行为主义的创始人约翰·华生 * 所解释的那样，"已知刺激，心理学能预测将会发生的反应，或者已知反应，能够说明有效刺激的性质。"[5] 这样的刺激可以是复杂的，比如一般环境的状况——例如，感受到屋子里的人不太友好，也可以是简单的，比如铃声。

许多学者认为，行为主义的一些观点已经成为心理学的核心，因为这门学科吸收了机能主义的一些观点。正如其中一位学者所写，"所有现代心理学家，只收集关于行为的经验证据，试图尽可能精确地阐明刺激与反应之间的规律性联系，（并且）对否定经验数据的理论持怀疑态度。"[6]但"证据"的定义仍不明确，许多认知科学家正在研究难以观察但可通过思想实验来概念化（一种根据结果提出假说的方法）的认知过程。

持续争议

　　尽管詹姆斯的《心理学原理》，作为历史产物比作为心理学探索的积极成果影响更深远，它也的确对现今一些流派有着启发作用，尤其在致力于提高我们对意识的理解的认知科学领域。尽管该学科尚未就确切构成意识的内容达成共识，但认知科学家仍在其"神经学和计算原理"的基础上继续研究。[7]认知心理学的主要问题一直是区分"人"的认知（有意识的）与人工智能（无意识的）。

　　英国计算机科学开拓者阿兰·图灵*提出了著名的"图灵测试"以区分人类智能（有意识的）和人工智能（无意识的）。测试中，测试者坐在电脑前，使用聊天软件与人或电脑对话。如果电脑成功让测试者认为其是人类，则可被视为有意识的。

　　这个观点可以通过哲学家约翰·塞尔*提出的"中国房间"的概念来论证。该实验让被测试者想象自己坐在一个房间里，房间里有一本代码本和代表某种语言的符号，而这种语言是被测试者不会说的一种语言（实验的目的语——汉语）。代码本提示哪些符号可以与哪些符号匹配。有人用代码语言写了一个问题，被测试者利用代码本可以给出答案。尽管不会汉语的人有可能依据一本写得足够好的代码本给出一个完美的答案，但我们并不能由此断定被测试者"理解"汉语。操纵符号的能力并不等同于认知力、感知力、理解力或思考能力。对于计算机而言，它的工作原理就是操纵符号，然而计算机运行程序的简单能力并不能说明其认知能力。[8] 塞尔认为，认知取决于精神内容：我们的大脑产生意识（思维认知、理解行为），这不只是单纯的过程，而是一种更高层次的思维活动。[9]

1. 杰拉尔德·E.迈尔斯："导论：背景知识"，威廉·詹姆斯著，《心理学原理》（第1—2卷），马萨诸塞州坎布里奇：哈佛大学出版社，1981年，第XIV页。
2. 迈尔斯："导论：背景知识"，第LXV页。
3. 戈登·奥尔波特："威廉·詹姆斯的生产悖论"，《心理学评论》第50卷，1943年第1期，第95页。
4. B. F. 斯金纳：引自B. R. 赫根汉，《心理学史导论》，贝尔蒙特：沃兹沃斯出版社，2009年，第445页。
5. 约翰·华生：引自约翰·A.米尔斯，《控制：行为心理学史》，纽约：纽约大学出版社，第9页。
6. 伯纳德·巴尔斯：引自赫根汉，《心理学史导论》，第412页。
7. 赫根汉：《心理学史导论》，第634页。
8. 见塞尔：引自赫根汉，《心理学史导论》，第630页。
9. 塞尔：引自赫根汉，《心理学史导论》，第630页。

12 未来展望

要点 🔑

- 尽管詹姆斯在撰写《心理学原理》时科学技术并不发达，但之后的研究者借助了现代科学的力量来证明和升华他的观点。
- 詹姆斯最突出的贡献可能是他的"意识流"概念，这一概念已被艺术家、科学家和公众所接受。
- 《心理学原理》不仅使心理学成为一门硬科学，还提出了一些重要概念，比如情绪的生理基础。

潜力

在那个时代，威廉·詹姆斯的《心理学原理》大大促进了关于大脑如何发展和工作的讨论。虽然 21 世纪的先进技术为科学家的研究提供了更高级的研究工具，但他们的结论与詹姆斯的一些见解仍非常吻合，尤其是大脑的结构和功能方面。

其中一些结论表明，即使没有技术帮助，詹姆斯的分析也是非常准确的。理查德·汤普森*在他的论文《学习和记忆的神经生物学：记忆中的威廉·詹姆斯》中指出，詹姆斯的作品对现代科学发现有着预示作用。汤普森指出，詹姆斯"表达了神经网络*中关于大脑定位*和可塑性的观点，这预示了当前神经生物学的许多方面"。[1]科学家发现大脑的某些部分操控着某些功能——他们称之为"定位"。这些功能包括语言、理性思维和视觉感觉。神经可塑性——大脑根据经验创造神经通路的想法——在某种程度上与詹姆斯关于习惯的研究有关，詹姆斯认为一个习惯可以由一个更强的习惯来替换。

> "我所谓'精神的我',是相对于经验自我而言的,并不是意识的一种过渡状态,我的意识状态,我的精神官能和性情的全部集合都是具体的。这个集合可以在任何时候成为我当时思想的对象,唤醒情感,就像那些被我的其他部分唤醒的情感。"
>
> —— 威廉·詹姆斯:《心理学原理》

未来方向

詹姆斯的主要观点对解释后辈心理学家研究的核心问题很有帮助,比如"什么是思想?""什么是意识?""'心灵'和'身体'之间是否有关系?"等一系列问题。但在很多方面,心理学也涉及隐喻性解释,如詹姆斯影响深远的"意识流"概念。

"意识流"的概念在其他非专业领域也被广泛应用,它一直是创造力的源泉。正如一位学者指出的,"艺术家们通过写作、电影甚至绘画来表现意识流,为我们自己的经验提供了试金石。"[2] 然而,这不仅仅是一个叙事隐喻。严谨的学者们仍在研究它,这些学者通过一股**创造性**意识流来研究白日梦、幻想和"日常的想象过程"。现代研究人员能通过尝试定位大脑半球之中的意识流获得詹姆斯无法获得的信息。他们还研究了意识流将人们从感官的日常世界中解放出来的方式。

小结

威廉·詹姆斯把心理学看作一种方式,这种方式能够弥补现代迫近的存在无意的状况。"社会情感、各种形式的玩乐、令人兴奋的艺术暗示、哲学沉思的趣味、宗教情感的残留、道德自我认同的喜悦、幻想和智慧的魅力——其中的一些或全部都是绝对必要的，这已经不仅仅是一个概念了。"[3] 这种让生存变得"可容忍"的愿望促使他将心理学确立为一门科学。但这不是一个快乐或满足的人说的话。

《心理学原理》彻底改变了心理学。詹姆斯有效地将其与哲学区分开来，而不像他的欧洲同行那样诉诸结构主义。他提出的概念，有些一直沿用至今。例如，他认为情绪不仅仅是从心理传递到身体，而是应该有两个层面的含义（看到一个怪物会让你的身体颤抖，你会因为颤抖而感到恐惧）。当然，他最重要的观点是"意识流"概念，这一观点认为，意识不是一些割裂的片段，而是一种川流不息的观感和心理状态。"意识流"除了使心理学产生重大变革，也为 20 世纪一些最著名的文学作品提供了灵感。

詹姆斯相信，我们"在任何时候都会尽可能多的满足需求"。他认为这证明了我们都在努力争取一个"更丰富的世界……变得极有组织性，更适于成为复杂结合体的一部分，更适于成为包容整体的一员"。[4]

1. 理查德·汤普森："学习和记忆的神经生物学：记忆中的威廉·詹姆斯"，《心理科学》第 1 卷，1990 年第 3 期，第 172 页。
2. 肯尼斯·S. 波普和杰罗姆·L. 辛格："引言：人类经验的流动"，肯尼斯·波普和杰罗姆·L. 辛格编，《意识流：人类经验流动的科学调查》，纽约：斯普林格出版社，1978 年，第 3 页。

3. 威廉·詹姆斯:《哲学论文集》，马萨诸塞州坎布里奇和伦敦：哈佛大学出版社，
1978 年，第 13 页。

4. 威廉·詹姆斯:《信仰的意志和通俗哲学论文集》，马萨诸塞州坎布里奇和伦敦：
哈佛大学出版社，1979 年，第 205、210 页。

术语表

1. **亚马孙河**：流经南美洲，是世界上最长的两条河流之一。许多文明在亚马孙盆地蓬勃发展，其中的一些文明至今仍十分神秘。

2. **行为主义**：一种心理学的研究方法，它建立在心理只能通过可观察的行为来理解这一概念之上。以 B. F. 斯金纳为代表的科学家们在 20 世纪早期发展了行为主义。

3. **资本主义**：在西方占主导地位的一种经济制度，资本家占有生产资料，剥削雇佣劳动，榨取剩余价值。

4. **认知科学**：研究大脑如何处理信息的跨学科领域。

5. **决定论**：一种认为我们的行为是由自然法则决定的学说。

6. **实证的**：通过观察可证实的。

7. **副现象说**：一种认为刺激，如外部事件或肌肉收缩等内部现象，都会引起心理事件（思想或感觉）的学说。

8. **经验主义**：在科学领域，依靠可控实验测试作为实验证据的观点。

9. **自由意志**：人类不以外部原因或神的旨意为转移的自由选择的概念。

10. **机能主义**：一种以现象在一个系统或有机体的持续运行中起重要作用的假设为基础的科学方法；在心理学中，机能主义理论认为心理过程与生物学要求有关或反映了人类物种的进化史。

11. **格式塔心理学**：把思想和行为当作一个整体而不是独立组成部分的一种思想流派。

12. **工业化**：始于 19 世纪早期的英国，西方世界的大部分地区从以农村为基础的农业经济转变为以城市为基础的制造业经济的过程。

13. **神经支配**：字面意义，受神经支配的肌肉运动。

14. **内省**：源自拉丁文，意思是"自我批评"：分析自我情绪和心理的过程。

15. **定位**：在神经生物学中，指确定大脑的各个区域与哪些情绪或行为有关的科学工作。

16. **唯物主义者**：认为物质是我们所经历的一切的基础（包括精神现象）的科学家和哲学家。

17. **形而上学**：与哲学的一个分支有关，其根源可以追溯到古希腊哲学家亚里士多德研究的存在和认知的基本问题。

18. **现代主义**：欧洲艺术思潮运动，向传统的创作形式与技巧提出了挑战，在 20 世纪初达到高潮。

19. **先天论**：在心理学中，这个概念指被植入我们大脑中与生俱来的某些技能和能力。

20. **神经网络**：也被称为"神经通路"，指一个人在经历或感受情绪时在大脑中形成的通道。

21. **神经学**：研究神经系统功能的医学分支。

22. **现象学**：20 世纪初由德国哲学家埃德蒙德·胡塞尔创立的哲学流派。现象学家主要研究意识和与意识行为相关的现象。

23. **生理学**：研究有机体及其器官的性质和功能的学科。

24. **一夫多妻制**：多配偶的制度。虽然一些社会和宗教仍实行一夫多妻制，但在许多发达国家，这种制度已被废除。

25. **实用主义**：1870 年左右在美国兴起的哲学运动。实用主义认为，思想适用于预测、解决问题和产生影响。

26. **精神分析法**：奥地利神经学家西格蒙德·弗洛伊德在 1890 年左右提出的一系列分析流程和技术。它试图把识别无意识的心理过程作为一种治愈精神障碍的方法。

27. **心理学**：研究人类心理和行为的科学。

28. **还原论**：一种认为一个整体可以参照它的组成元素来理解的学说。通常人们用贬损的方式来讨论那些不考虑"整体情况"的复杂问题，但并非总是如此。

29. **文艺复兴**：欧洲文化史上的一个时期，通常为 14 世纪到 16 世纪，在这个时期，艺术家们通过古罗马和希腊的艺术表现形式来复兴欧洲文化。

30. **第二次工业革命**：工业化的扩张，开始于 1870 年左右，当时电动机器使生产进一步自动化。

31. **意识流**：由威廉·詹姆斯首创的概念，与意识（和无意识）的思想流动有关。

32. **结构主义**：20 世纪初兴起的一种思想流派，它试图把实体视为一个整体，而不是其组成部分。

33. **斯韦登堡主义**：1787 年在英国发起的基督教宗教运动，其信仰来源于瑞典科学家兼神学家伊曼纽尔·斯韦登堡的著作。

34. **离群索居**：在地理、生理和文化层面上，所有熟悉的事物被去除的感觉。

人名表

1. **吉恩·路易斯·阿加西斯**（1807—1873），瑞士生物学家和地质学家，他对自然科学的许多贡献都因反对达尔文主义而被掩盖。

2. **戈登·奥尔波特**（1897—1967），美国心理学家，拒绝精神病学和行为主义，将个人视为独一无二的个体（"人格心理学"）。

3. **詹姆斯·安吉尔**（1869—1949），美国心理学家，因在耶鲁大学时期所做的研究而闻名，是功能主义的关键人物（从心理学角度来看，心理过程是建立在生物需求之上的）。

4. **亚里士多德**（公元前384—公元前322），柏拉图的学生，古希腊最重要的哲学家之一，他的名字被收入《大英百科全书》，他被称为"历史上第一位真正的科学家"。

5. **詹姆斯·卡特尔**（1860—1944），美国心理学家，美国第一位心理学教授，在他的帮助下，心理学被确立为一门真正的科学。

6. **让-马丁·沙可**（1825—1893），法国神经学家，常被认为是现代神经学之父。

7. **查尔斯·达尔文**（1809—1882），英国博物学家和地质学家，以其1859年的著作《物种起源》中的进化论而闻名。

8. **勒内·笛卡尔**（1596—1650），法国哲学家、数学家和科学家。他被许多人认为是西方哲学之父，并因"我思故我在"这句话而被人们铭记。

9. **约翰·杜威**（1859—1952），美国哲学家、心理学家和教育改革家。学者们认为他是功能心理学的奠基人之一。

10. **西格蒙德·弗洛伊德**（1856—1939），奥地利神经学家，被世人誉为精神分析学之父，研究无意识心理的治疗和理论研究方法。

11. **罗素·古德曼**，新墨西哥大学研究威廉·詹姆斯的知名学术权威。

12. **赫尔曼·冯·亥姆霍兹**（1821—1894），德国内科医生，他因在人类感觉系统方面的研究而闻名。

13. **沙德沃思·霍尔韦·霍奇森**（1832—1912），英国哲学家。詹姆斯认为他是实用主义的创始人。

14. **大卫·休谟**（1711—1776），苏格兰哲学家、历史学家和经济学家，因其对经验主义、自然主义和怀疑论的影响而闻名。

15. **埃德蒙德·胡塞尔**（1859—1938），德国哲学家，现象学奠基人。

16. **亨利·詹姆斯**（1843—1916），威廉的弟弟，小说家和文学评论家。他一生大部分时间都在英国度过，他的许多作品，包括《鸽子的翅膀》（1902）和《金碗》（1904），都提及了欧洲人和美国人的性格对比。

17. **詹姆斯·乔伊斯**（1882—1941），爱尔兰小说家和诗人，因其颇具影响力的现代主义文学风格而闻名。

18. **伊曼努尔·康德**（1724—1804），德国哲学家，被公认为现代哲学的核心人物。他的作品对后世许多哲学家都有启示作用。

19. **卡尔·兰格**（1834—1900），丹麦医生，对神经学、精神病学和心理学做出了重大贡献。

20. **约翰·洛克**（1632—1704），英国医生和经验主义哲学家。他提出了"心智理论"，促生了现代的身份和自我概念。

21. **C. S. 皮尔斯**（1839—1914），美国哲学家。他在许多领域都做出了重大贡献，并作为逻辑学家和实用主义的创始人闻名。

22. **柏拉图**（约公元前427—公元前348），古代最重要的哲学家之一，他的著作为科学和西方哲学研究奠定了基础。

23. **马塞尔·普鲁斯特**（1871—1922），法国小说家和评论家，因其七卷小说《追忆逝水年华》而为人所熟知。

24. **伯特兰·罗素**（1872—1970），英国哲学家和政治活动家，与其门生路德维希·维特根斯坦等人一起创立了分析哲学学派。

25. 乔治·桑塔亚纳（1863—1952），西班牙裔哲学家，诗歌、小说和散文作家，文化评论家。

26. 约翰·塞尔（1932 年生），美国的哲学家和学者，他最著名的作品涉及语言哲学和心灵哲学。

27. B. F. 斯金纳（1904—1990），美国心理学家，新行为主义学派的领军人物之一。

28. 理查德·汤普森（1930—2014），世界顶尖的神经学家之一。他在学习记忆科学上做了许多开创性工作。

29. E. L. 桑戴克（1874—1949），美国心理学家，研究比较心理学和人们如何学习。

30. 阿兰·图灵（1912—1954），英国计算机科学家的先驱，他在二战期间破译了德国的"谜码"，为大众所熟知。学者们认为他是人工智能之父。

31. 约翰·华生（1878—1958），美国心理学家，行为主义学派的创始人。

32. 路德维希·维特根斯坦（1889—1951），奥地利裔英国哲学家，主要研究逻辑、心理哲学和语言。尽管他一生中很少发表著作，但他死后出版的合集《哲学研究》仍然是 20 世纪最重要的哲学著作之一。

33. 弗吉尼亚·伍尔芙（1882—1941），英国小说家、散文家、评论家，现代主义文学领军人物。

34. 威廉·冯特（1832—1920），德国医生、哲学家和心理学家，他是第一个将心理学与生物学和哲学区分开来的人。

WAYS IN TO THE TEXT

KEY POINTS

- William James (1842–1910) was an American psychologist,* philosopher, and physiologist.* "Psychology" is the study of the human mind and behavior; "physiology" is the study of the nature and functioning of bodily organs.

- *The Principles of Psychology* (1890) sets out to bring philosophical ideas about our minds and behavior into the realm of empirical* (evidence-based) science.

- While *The Principles of Psychology* is a foundational text of the discipline of psychology, its influences are now felt across many different disciplines, including the arts and literature.

Who Was William James?

William James, the author of *The Principles of Psychology* (1890), was born in 1842 in New York City. His brother, Henry James,* was a prominent American novelist. The two were close, and benefited from the intellectual environment of their childhood home. Growing up with two other brothers and a sister, the James boys who would achieve the greatest prominence "learned that not to question and to have no opinion was to shirk not only one's intellectual duty but one's moral responsibilities."[1] As a result, both Henry and William focused on their chosen fields (literature and psychology, respectively) with observant, clever styles, centered on art and artistry.

William James spent his teens in the Swiss city of Geneva and in Paris and Boulogne-sur-Mer in France, studying science, among other subjects. He moved back to the US in 1858 to study painting in Newport, Rhode Island. Having divided his time between studying science in Europe and painting in Newport, he eventually settled on medical science, enrolling at Harvard in 1861. Four years later, he joined the Swiss biologist Jean Louis Agassiz,* his teacher in medicine, on an expedition up the Amazon River.* In the following years, he also had the opportunity to study under the noted physicians Wilhelm Wundt* and Hermann von Helmholtz* in Germany; both were engaged in early research in the field of psychology, which served to stimulate his interest in the subject. After completing his studies at Harvard, he established the first American psychology laboratory in 1874. James began working on *The Principles of Psychology* in 1878.

James continued working on *The Principles of Psychology* throughout the 1880s, publishing it in 1890. During this period, he also taught psychology and philosophy at Harvard. *Principles* remains his most important work. He revisited many of the same physical and psychological issues in subsequent works including *The Will to Believe and Other Essays in Popular Philosophy* (1897), *The Varieties of Religious Experience*, and late writings including *Pragmatism* (1907), *A Pluralistic Universe* (1909), and *Essays in Radical Empiricism* (1912). James died in 1910.

What Does *The Principles of Psychology* Say?

In *The Principles of Psychology*, James attempts to establish psychology as a science; he defines this as "the description and explanation of states of consciousness as such."[2] He sought to use introspection*—that is, "looking into our minds and reporting what we there discover"—to speculate on the relationship between our mental activity and our physical bodies, particularly the structure of our brains.[3]

Principles remains significant in the history of psychology because of James's attempt to unify otherwise isolated scientific styles into a unified whole; a philosopher and a doctor, he sought to connect philosophical ideas with biology and medicine.

One of the most important ideas James articulates in *Principles* centers on the "stream of consciousness,"* a term he coined himself. He held that all thoughts occur, one after the other, and in relation to one another, and he uses the metaphor of a stream to illustrate the concept. For James, this continual stream of thought *was* consciousness—constant reflection, self-reflection, creativity, sensation, and so forth—all jumbled together. Other psychologists tended to split mental states into their composite parts; they might think of a yellow ball as a color, a shape, and a concept, for example, rather than as a whole "thought."

James also believed the physical and the mental were uniquely entwined. He argued that emotions and habits did not exist simply as mental states but resulted from interactions between the mind, the brain, and the physical body. For example, he believed that emotions resulted from changes in the body—the speeding of a heartbeat, or the flushing of a face—as interpreted by the mind. James also believed that people could control their emotions if they forced themselves to act in a certain way.

But at the core of *Principles*, James attempts to liberate the mind and its inner workings. In this, he contrasted with the more mechanical thought of earlier philosophers such as eighteenth-century Scottish philosopher David Hume* and his German follower Immanuel Kant.* Where Hume and Kant sought to understand the mind in terms of perfect rationality, considering its operations in terms of calculation, James seeks a richer understanding of human experience. By observing how we act, he wants to bring psychology, with all its imperfection and humanity, into its own as a discipline distinct from philosophy.

Why Does *The Principles of Psychology* Matter?

More than 125 years after its publication, the blend of philosophy, physiology, and psychology in *The Principles of Psychology* continues to influence how we think. It remains important to the discipline of psychology, of course—but it also stands as a milestone in intellectual history. This book legitimized psychology as an independent science, distinct from biology or chemistry. It also provided a major motivation for the growing interest in psychological exploration in America and Europe during the late nineteenth century.

Principles has been so influential that many consider James "the father of American psychology." While psychology and its associated fields have made considerable progress over the last century, meaning that students no longer read *Principles* as a scientific textbook, its impact on the discipline of psychology remains undeniable. The work must be considered a crucial contribution to intellectual history.

Beyond psychology, it has proven influential in the

discipline of philosophy, having inspired later movements including pragmatism* (an approach that considers the practical applications of philosophical inquiry to be paramount) and phenomenology* (roughly, inquiry into the nature and roles of perception and experience in the formation and expression of consciousness). With *Principles*, James singlehandedly influenced generations of intellectuals in both America and Europe, including prominent philosophers like the US thinker John Dewey,* the British philosopher and social activist Bertrand Russell,* and the Austrian British philosopher of language and mind Ludwig Wittgenstein.*The introspective and artistic nature of James's insights in *Principles* also influenced modern art and literature. Artists—particularly writers—have been fascinated with the psychological concepts he outlined. Perhaps most significantly, James's concept of the "stream of consciousness" became important in understanding how modernist* writers created novels and short stories ("modernism" was a movement in the arts and architecture of the early twentieth century that challenged traditional forms). Indeed, his "stream of consciousness" may be more famous as a literary device than as a psychological concept. Writers such as James Joyce,* the author of *Ulysses* (1922), Virginia Woolf,* the author of *The Waves* (1931), and Marcel Proust,* author of *À la recherche du temps perdu* (1913–27), all employed variants of the idea in their work.

The Principles of Psychology has had an undeniably profound impact on the world of ideas.

1. Eugene Taylor, "Oh Those Fabulous James Boys!," *Psychology Today*, December 15, 2011, accessed December 17, 2015, https: //www. psychologytoday.com/articles/199503/oh-those-fabulous-james-boys.

2. William James, *Psychology: Briefer Course* (Cambridge, MA, and London: Harvard University Press, 1984), 1.

3. William James, *The Principles of Psychology*, *Vols 1–2* (Cambridge, MA: Harvard University Press, 1981), 185.

SECTION 1
INFLUENCES

THE AUTHOR AND THE HISTORICAL CONTEXT

KEY POINTS

- *The Principles of Psychology* remains a very important work in the history of Western psychology* (the science of the human mind and behavior).

- James's childhood, adolescence, and coming-of-age in New York City were influenced by the Christian movement of Swedenborgism,* followed by his father, and the urban intellectualism of both his parents.

- By the late nineteenth century, it seemed increasingly clear to many thinkers like James that traditional disciplines such as philosophy and even relatively new sciences such as biology failed to explain the mind.

Why Read This Text?

With his 1890 text, *The Principles of Psychology*, William James helped to solidify the new discipline of psychology as a bridge between the human and the natural sciences. Already a well-known name, with its publication James deepened his reputation as a preeminent figure in the new discipline of psychology.

James's influence also extended outside this discipline, however. "Stream of consciousness,"* a phrase he coined to describe the way that consciousness was formed by a flow of reflection, observation, and recollection, has since been used much more extensively in literary contexts. Prominent authors such as the early twentieth-century writers James Joyce,*Virginia Woolf,* and Marcel Proust* of Ireland, England, and France, respectively, applied the concept in their writings. One writer remarks that,"the novels that are said to use the stream-of-consciousness technique to a considerable degree prove, upon analysis, to be novels which have as their essential subject matter the consciousness of one or more characters ... the depicted consciousness serves as a screen on which the material in these novels is presented."[1]

It is hard to overestimate the impact *Principles* has had on Western psychology. Critics rightly celebrate it as James's central text. Contemporary scholars remind us of its unparalleled importance in history when they openly praise James as the most influential American philosopher and psychologist of the late nineteenth and early twentieth centuries.[2]

> "The huge human brain, approximately 1, 350 cubic centimeters, is the most complex organic structure in the known world."
> —— David M. Buss, Foundations of *Evolutionary Psychology*

Author's Life

William James was born in New York City on January 11, 1842. His father was a wealthy follower of Swedenborgism, the religious movement founded by the Swedish scientist and religious mystic Emanuel Swedenborg, and his mother was a sophisticated member of New York's upper classes. He received his early education primarily through tutors and private schools as the family moved frequently between Europe and America. This constant movement left young James feeling rootless and isolated.

James entered the Lawrence Scientific School at Harvard in 1861 and began studying at Harvard's School of Medicine in 1864. After embarking on an academic expedition to the Amazon* and spending time in Europe, James returned to medical school in 1866 and received his medical degree in 1869.

While in Europe in 1868, James had the opportunity to study with Wilhelm Wundt* and Hermann von Helmholtz,* German physicians who were both interested in the human mind, prompting an interest in psychology.[3] In 1872, James accepted an offer to teach undergraduate courses in comparative physiology* at Harvard, and by 1874, he was not only teaching anatomy and physiology, but also psychology. The university appointed him an assistant professor of philosophy in 1880, two years after he married Alice Howe Gibbens.

James's work as a teacher of psychology and philosophy throughout the 1880s informed the writing of *Principles.* By 1890, *Principles*, his most significant work, was finally ready for publication. He would revisit many of the same issues—especially the relationship between the physical and psychological—in subsequent publications. Among these were *The Will to Believe and Other Essays in Popular Philosophy* (1897), *The Varieties of Religious Experience* (which is based on lectures he gave between 1901 and 1902), and a number of late writings: *Pragmatism* (1907), *A Pluralistic Universe* (1909), and *Essays in Radical Empiricism* (1912).

Author's Background

For James, the most important historical events that influenced *Principles* occurred as part of the Second Industrial Revolution.* Preindustrial Europe had an agricultural economy. People lived in villages, growing enough food to feed themselves, and paid taxes to their local lords. The First Industrial Revolution—which began in the eighteenth century—introduced a process of economic and social transformation with its roots in Western Europe. As new methods of production evolved—such as steam-powered machines to produce goods—this way of life was transformed. People began to work for wages in cities, and those cities became increasingly connected by steam-powered trains and boats. Capitalism,* in which trade and industry are conducted for the sake of private profit, became the main economic system of the West.

The Second Industrial Revolution began in James's time, the late nineteenth century. The First Industrial Revolution had concentrated production in a few centers, with easy access to the coal needed to run its machinery. But the invention of electricity allowed factories to spring up virtually anywhere in the developed world. As a result, an unprecedented number of people moved from farms to cities, and between cities. Uprooted from their traditional communities and support structures, workers found themselves in unfamiliar situations. This sense of uprootedness* affected members of the working class in ways that had to be understood psychologically;privileged intellectuals such as James sought to explain what was happening.

In *Principles*, James attempts to unravel the mystery of human experience while doing justice to its complexity. In the process, he supported the creation of psychology as a scientific discipline in the United States.

---

1. Robert Humphrey, *Stream of Consciousness in the Modern Novel: A Study of James Joyce, Virginia Woolf, Dorothy Richardson, William Faulkner and Others* (Berkeley: University of California Press, 1968), 2.

2. David Buss, *Evolutionary Psychology: The New Science of the Mind* (Boston: Pearson, 2008), 2–35.

3. Stephanie L. Hawkins, "William James, Gustav Fechner, and Early Psychophysics," *Frontiers in Physiology* 2 (2011): 68, accessed February 2016, doi: 10.3389/fphys.2011.00068.

MODULE 2
ACADEMIC CONTEXT

KEY POINTS

* An interdisciplinary work, *The Principles of Psychology* combines psychology,* philosophy, and physiology.*

* James's work can be seen as the next step in a line of inquiry stretching back to the ancient Greeks, as well as Renaissance* philosophers like the French thinker Descartes* and his intellectual descendants (the Renaissance was the period, following the medieval period, in which European culture was reinvigorated by a turn towards the artistic and architectural models of ancient Roman and Greece).

* James was deeply influenced by psychology and philosophy, and by the English naturalist Charles Darwin,* whose work was vital to the development of modern evolutionary theory.

The Work in its Context

Before William James wrote *The Principles of Psychology*, scholars debated the status of the discipline of psychology. Generally, they saw the discipline as falling somewhere between science and philosophy and a field of inquiry "characterized by a rich diversity of methods, topics of interest, and assumptions about human nature."[1] It is often understood as not being concerned with the nature of arms or legs, or even necessarily of *brains*, but rather of minds; as a discipline, many see psychology as concerned with the mental life of people—their ideas, their motivations.

Can such a philosophical concept of a mind be investigated as a science? Science, after all, is based on empirical* data—

information verifiable by observation. So how can one investigate a "mind"? Indeed, where in the body does the mind reside? When James wrote *The Principles of Psychology*, scholars were gradually accepting the field as a science that investigated the mind and spirit, but they still wrestled with questions about psychology's area of inquiry, its categories, and its methods of investigation.

> "This preservation of favourable individual differences and variations, and the destruction of those which are injurious, I have called Natural Selection, or the Survival of the Fittest."
>
> ——Charles Darwin, *On the Origin of Species*

Overview of the Field

At least as far back as the ancient Greeks, scholars have been analyzing their own mental states. The ancient Greek philosopher Plato* suggested that each human's imperfect body was inhabited by a rational soul—a soul with knowledge of perfectly rational things. According to Plato, a material object such as a table was an imperfect reflection of the essential form of a table that existed outside of nature. For later philosophers, such as Plato's student Aristotle,* however, one could determine what "tableness" was by investigating enough tables to make a rational inference.[2]

Over a millennium later in Renaissance Europe, thinkers like the French philosopher René Descartes tried to consider precisely what the mind was. Descartes declared that only humans possess a mind, and that mind is a nonphysical aspect of ourselves, "that provided consciousness, free choice, and rationality."[3] Descartes's most famous saying, "I think therefore I am," describes this process. Descartes can be confident in his own existence, at least as a mind, because he engages in the activity of thinking. From this, Descartes concluded that a nonphysical mind controls a physical body (this is "dualism," the principle that humanity is made of minds and bodies). Driven by rational minds, humans are machines of meat holding "innate" ideas.

Empiricists like the seventeenth-century English philosopher John Locke* made the opposite point. Locke likened the mind to a blank sheet of white paper, which gets colored in when we sense things in the real world. Everything is material: ideas merely represent sensory experiences reflected on our brains. In the eighteenth century, the Scottish philosopher David Hume* argued that behavior results only from our passions (that is, emotions), and we act largely deterministically*—our actions are determined by natural laws. All we have are our sensations and our robotic reactions to them: a passive mind, battered about by circumstances.

Academic Influences

The thinkers outlined above are all, more or less, properly called philosophers. Philosophy influenced James deeply, but he was also drawn to psychology and the natural sciences. Studying under the physicians Wilhelm Wundt* and Hermann von Helmholtz* in Germany fed his keen interest in psychology.

The English naturalist Charles Darwin exerted an equally powerful influence. Darwin proposed the theory of evolution by natural selection, a theory essentially arguing that individuals who are better adapted to their environments remain more likely to survive and reproduce, passing on their traits to the next generation. James believed Darwin's ideas could apply to the behavior and characteristics of organisms by inferring that they are "adaptive" in some way. James introduced a concept called functionalism* that extended Darwinian principles to the study of the mind. Functional characteristics improve an organism's ability to reproduce—that is a basic principle of natural selection. Since we are the product of evolution, our behaviors and mental states have some connection to our biology and must have been shaped by the necessity to adapt to the environment. This does not imply that James was a pure materialist*—only that he believed consciousness has a functional purpose in adapting to an environment.[4]

---

1. B. R. Hergenhahn, *An Introduction to the History of Psychology* (Belmont: Wadsworth, 2009), 2.

2. Hergenhahn, *Introduction*, 49–50.

3. Hergenhahn, *Introduction*, 121.

4. For more on James's debt to Darwin, see Robert J. Richards, "The Personal Equation in Science: William James's Psychological and Moral Uses of the Darwinian Theory," in *A William James Renaissance: Four Essays by Young Scholars*, ed. Mark R. Schwehn, *Harvard Library Bulletin* 30, no. 4 (1982): 387–425.

MODULE 3
THE PROBLEM

KEY POINTS

• In James's time, most people felt that psychology,* although fascinating, had still not established itself as a science.

• Building on the arguments and assumptions of the psychologists and philosophers who preceded him, James introduced several original concepts.

• James renewed fundamental questions such as "What is experience?" and "Can introspection*—investigating one's own mental process—reveal insight into the psyche and its physical traces?"

Core Question

William James's *The Principles of Psychology* asks how we can discover and systematically elaborate on the foundational laws that define the science of psychology. He explores the nature of the mind, and whether we may understand it as something "real" and with purpose. He inquires about the nature of consciousness and the nature of a thought. The answers to these questions distinguish psychology from other modes of inquiry: where chemistry is concerned with physical matter and biology concerned with organisms, for example, psychology is concerned with mental states.

The Principles of Psychology redefines the usual questions of mind and body. It breaks from previous styles of investigation, through James's original use of introspection, a concept he understood as "looking into our own minds and reporting what we there discover."[1] This method of self-reflexive thinking becomes particularly apparent in chapters such as "The Functions of the Brain" and "On Some General Conditions of Brain Activity." James's nuanced, introspective analysis of the physical traces of the individual and his or her spirit lies at the heart of *The Principles of Psychology*. But the precise method of psychology had still to be defined. So *The Principles of Psychology* necessarily had to confront an elusive object of study. Even James's most capable colleagues had not been able to pin down the exact nature of psychology.

James was not the first to struggle to establish an entirely new discipline, as he makes explicit in the lengthy chapter on the self in which he discusses the thought of the eighteenth-century philosophers David Hume* and Immanuel Kant.* But he also retrieves thoughts from as far back as ancient Greek philosophers like Plato.*These forebears helped James lay the intellectual foundations for the new discipline of psychology, and for his enduringly influential book. *The Principles of Psychology* galvanized the new field of psychology and bolstered the discipline's legitimacy as a new modern science.

> "The definition of Psychology may be best given ... as the description and explanation of states of consciousness as such. By states of consciousness are meant such things as sensations, desires, emotions, cognitions, reasonings, decisions, volitions, and the like. Their 'explanation' must of course include the study of their causes, conditions, and immediate consequences, so far as these can be ascertained."
>
> —— William James, *The Principles of Psychology*

The Participants

Many consider the German physician, physiologist,* and philosopher Wilhelm Wundt* a cofounder of psychology. Like James, Wundt sought to establish psychology as a science apart from biology and philosophy. He built the first laboratory for psychological research at the University of Leipzig. Wundt represented a more experimentalist* school of psychology. He believed that we could understand thought through experimental analysis—by breaking it down into its component parts. In Wundt's view, reducing consciousness to its basic components (reactions, sensations, and so on) allows us to understand its motions—a point of view James argued against. Considering the whole in terms of a system defined by its components is an approach termed "structuralism."*

Another school of thought against which James wrote was epiphenomenalism,* according to which the "the brain causes mental events, but mental events cannot cause behavior."[2] This is crucial because it is an entirely material understanding of mental states: consciousness remains irrelevant, because it does not cause anything. Epiphenomenalists compare consciousness to the whistle on a steam train. The whistle blows before the train leaves, but the whistle has no impact on the train's movement. The English philosopher Shadworth Holloway Hodgson* was a prominent advocate of this point of view.

The Contemporary Debate

James and his contemporaries debated what consciousness

is and how we ought to understand it. In *Principles*, James responded directly to both Wundt's theory and to Hodgson's epiphenomenalism. He rejected epiphenomenalism, suggesting it was based on an unprovable and unrealistic notion."To urge the automaton-theory upon us," he noted, the epiphenomenalists make no empirical* argument. In fact, the argument they do make runs counter to common sense and shuts down debate: it is "an unwarrantable impertinence in the present state of psychology."[3]

James calls structuralism a "microscopic psychology ... carried on by experimental methods."[4] For him, it uses the method of introspection, but through the use of statistics. Ultimately, James believed structuralism asked the wrong questions. "Bent on studying the elements of the mental life, dissecting them from the [greater] results in which they are embedded," he writes, it reduces them to mere "quantitative scales."[5] Ultimately, James thought ideas could not be investigated like this. In his view, they simply do not lend themselves to being compared and quantified.

---

1. William James, *The Principles of Psychology*, *Vols 1–2* (Cambridge, MA: Harvard University Press, 1981), 185.
2. B. R. Hergenhahn, *An Introduction to the History of Psychology* (Belmont: Wadsworth, 2009), 18.
3. James, *Principles*, 141.
4. James, *Principles*, 192–3.
5. James, *Principles*, 192–3.

MODULE 4
THE AUTHOR'S CONTRIBUTION

KEY POINTS

* In *The Principles of Psychology*, James primarily aimed to facilitate acceptance of psychology* as a scientific discipline.
* The author's argument about the scientific nature of psychology initiated a new analysis of experience.
* *The Principles of Psychology* incorporated and built on both the works of previous philosophers and psychologists and on James's own earlier work.

Author's Aims

In *The Principles of Psychology*, William James set out to discover the scientific nature of such concepts as stream of consciousness* (the flow of recollections, observations, and reflections that together constitute the conscious mind), self-consciousness (awareness that one is conscious), emotion, and will. His analyses of these concepts helped to establish psychology as a legitimate science. The work highlighted the uniquely significant phenomena that psychology can unveil. James established himself as a founder of the American branch of the field of psychology by exploring mental experience both more deeply and more empirically* than anyone who came before.

For centuries, philosophers have debated the nature of the body and the mind. James's work brings this age-old discussion into the realm of the new discipline of psychology; in the fashion of traditional philosophy, however, he holds the position that "only as reflection becomes developed do we become aware of an inner world at all."[1]

Just before *The Principles of Psychology*'s publication in 1890, James confessed to his editor that the work did not offer a clear, systematic view of what the science of psychology presently was, nor what it should become. Nevertheless, scholars recognized its originality and value. James's greatest work, it remains relevant more than a century later. Its insights offer an understanding of the internal turmoil of the modern individual. Even as industrialization*—the process by which we turn from societies and economies founded on agriculture—alienates humans from nature and society, psychological knowledge gives each of us the power to deal with his or her own situation.

> *"For the places thus first sensibly known are elements of the child's space-world which remain with him all his life."*
> —— William James, *The Principles of Psychology*

Approach

The Principles of Psychology builds on ancient and recent philosophy and the work conducted in the field of psychology by James's contemporaries. The text breaks from both traditions, however, by harnessing the power of introspection* to shed new light on personal experience.

Introspection is the examination of our own experiences—sounds, images, impressions—in terms of what they have meant to ourself. James invites us to consider the deeper meaning of our thoughts—and the language we use to express them—as psychological data, remarking, for example, that "The rhythm of a lost word may be there without a sound to clothe it ... Everyone must know the tantalizing effect of the blank rhythm of some forgotten verse, restlessly dancing in one's mind, striving to be filled out with words."[2]

While James's methods may appear highly personal and philosophical, he was ultimately a pragmatist* (pragmatism was a school according to which "any belief, thought, or behavior must be judged by its consequences").[3] In other words, the main criterion of an idea's validity remains the extent to which it is useful. For a pragmatist, the "only test of probable truth is what works best in the way of leading us, what fits every part of life best and combines with the collectivity of experience's demands, nothing being omitted."[4]

James's pragmatism leads him to reject the spiritual idea of the "soul." In his view, one cannot "deduce any of the properties of the mental life from otherwise known properties of the soul." Someone with a desire to know the world or to enjoy freedom would have to find "various characters ready-made in the mental life, and [clap these] into the Soul."[5] When we can identify mental states such as pleasure or hunger that do not require an eternal soul, what do we have to gain from our analysis by considering the existence of a soul at all?

Contribution in Context

The Principles of Psychology laid the foundation for psychology to be recognized as a legitimate science uniting philosophical and biological concepts. James's book contributed significantly to this recognition. But his work did not appear in a vacuum. The works of philosophers, biologists, and others interested in the study of psychology all influenced his thinking. Certainly, Charles Darwin's* theory of evolution contributed greatly to James's concept of functionalism*—the principle that our mental processes have specific functions related to our evolutionary history. And James's studies with the German physicians Willem Wundt* and Hermann von Helmholtz* shaped his own interest in psychology.

James's own writings from several years before the publication of *The Principles of Psychology* hinted at some of the concepts he would cover in the text. In 1878, for instance, James discussed the relationship between mental states and external stimuli. He noted that the "mere correspondence with the outer world is a notion on which it is wholly impossible to base a definition of mental action."[6] James argued that mental states are internal affairs, and they act on the outside world; they cannot be understood exclusively as responses to external stimuli. Seeing the world from the perspective of the inside-out, rather than the outside-in, is called "nativism"*; the idea has its roots in James's earlier work.

---

1. William James, *The Principles of Psychology*, *Vols 1-2* (Cambridge, MA: Harvard University Press, 1981), 679.

2. James, *Principles*, 244.

3. B. R. Hergenhahn, *An Introduction to the History of Psychology* (Belmont: Wadsworth, 2009), 346.

4. William James, *Pragmatism* (New York: Dover Publications, 1907), 39.

5. James, *Principles*, 328–9.

6. William James, "Remarks on Spencer's Definition of Mind as Correspondence," *Journal of Speculative Philosophy* 12, no. 1 (1878): 13.

SECTION 2
IDEAS

MODULE 5
MAIN IDEAS

KEY POINTS

* *The Principles of Psychology* explores how thoughts and feelings connect with the physical brain.

* James coined the phrase "stream of consciousness"* to reflect the way thoughts move independently through the mind.

* James argued that psychology* deserves to be developed as a modern science and facilitated its transition into an accepted academic discipline.

Key Themes

William James's *The Principles of Psychology* offers a vision of psychology as a discipline that can reveal the mystery and dynamic nature of an individual's psyche. The psyche exists somewhere between the internal world, where one experiences states of mind, and the external world—the world of things that occupy those states of mind; "assuming that thoughts and feelings exist and are vehicles of knowledge," James argues that those thoughts and feelings connect with states of being in the physical brain.[1] But this does not mean that the mind merely emerges from physical twitches of the brain; "minds inhabit environments which act on them and on which they in turn react."[2]

"Body" is not one thing and "mind" another; rather, humans can be understood as an integrated mixture of the two. In this light, the work deals with states of mind and the correspondence between the outside world and those states of mind.

James deals with sensations and perceptions. We may define "sensation" as the process by which we collect sensory information from the external world;"perception" represents the way in which we interpret and understand sensory information. To put it another way, the "visual sensation of the gorilla may be that of a large, colored shape, whereas your perception of it includes more sensations around it, its relation to other things" and one's personal experience of gorillas.[3]

> "Consciousness, then, does not appear to itself chopped up in bits ... A 'river' or a 'stream' are the metaphors by which it is most naturally described. In talking of it hereafter, let us call it the stream of thought, of consciousness, or of subjective life."
>
> —— William James, *The Principles of Psychology*

Exploring the Ideas

While it remains difficult to pick out a single "key idea," we may fairly describe the work as an account of what consciousness is. Does consciousness arise from the body in the way that a rumble in the belly (external) might define what goes on in the mind (internal)? Or is it something purely innate—something intrinsic and inherent? For James, consciousness is not something that emerges from sensations (seeing a color, feeling a sting) and intensifies from there: rather, it both *is* and *arises from* thought. In other words, James does not aim to analyze sensing—which could be an entirely mechanical process; he wants to understand thinking itself.

This brings us to James's famous "stream of consciousness." "Such words as 'chain' or 'train' do not," James argues about consciousness, "describe it fitly as it presents itself in the first instance. It is nothing jointed; it flows."[4] James argues that thoughts are not made up of other sensations: he cannot reduce thinking about a yellow ball to a combination of the color yellow, a circle, the concept of a ball and its use, and so on. For one thing, imagining the yellow ball remains a completely personal act; it cannot be reduced to any component. And the thought does not just happen and disappear; it remains part of a continuous flow of ideas, or in James's metaphor, a stream.

If all thoughts arise and pass away in the context of one another, then "the rush of the thought is so headlong that it almost always brings us up at the conclusion before we can arrest it."[5] In other words, thoughts are not individual objects that can be taken, examined, and understood by reducing them to their elements (an approach called "reductionism").* Instead, "thought" remains a constant, part of a flowing stream that changes yet keeps moving. If I have one thought of a yellow ball and then another, they are not the same thought; they remain two distinct thoughts occurring in sequence.

James describes consciousness as a "theatre of simultaneous possibilities" which weights thoughts selectively and chooses to retain the most useful. When it comes to individual thoughts, consciousness can choose "the selection of some, and the suppression of the rest by the reinforcing and inhibiting agency of attention."[6] This helps us cope with a complex world demanding our attention.[7]

Language and Expression

The Principles of Psychology remains something of a curiosity in terms of its language and expression. While James usually writes with an admirable clarity, some passages remain obscure. Although he is not always clear about the overall structure of the book, many readers have found the absence of a key idea to be ironically productive. Even without this structural clarity, one can follow most of the author's observations, even the more esoteric and nuanced ones. At the least, it remains clear that James intends to illuminate the foundational laws of this new modern science.

James makes such compelling arguments in *The Principles of Psychology* that he managed to legitimize psychology as an academic discipline. Even though he deals with details of individual thought—phenomena that remain notoriously difficult to describe—his powers of communication shine through.

For an overwhelming number of scholars, *The Principles of Psychology* remains a foundational text in the field of psychological studies. It undoubtedly established psychology as a modern science. To be sure, the text has encountered criticism[8]— even from the author himself in a letter of 1890[9]—but no other text did as much to cement the early popularity and acclaim that psychology had just begun to enjoy in the United States and Europe.

1. William James, *The Principles of Psychology*, *Vols 1–2* (Cambridge, MA: Harvard University Press, 1981), VI.

2. James, *Principles*, 6.

3. Gerald E. Myers, "Introduction: The Intellectual Context," in James, *Principles of Psychology*, XXII-XXIII.

4. James, *Principles*, 239.

5. James, *Principles*, 244.

6. James, *Principles*, 288.

7. B. R. Hergenhahn, *An Introduction to the History of Psychology* (Belmont: Wadsworth, 2009), 341.

8. See, for example, William J. Gavin, *William James in Focus: Willing to Believe* (Bloomington: Indiana University Press, 2013); Michael Slater, *William James on Ethics and Faith* (Cambridge: Cambridge University Press, 2009); Michael Johnson and Tracy Henley, eds, *Reflections on* The Principles of Psychology: *William James After a Century* (Hillsdale, NJ: Lawrence Erlbaum Associates, 1990); James Pawelski, *The Dynamic Individualism of William James* (Albany, NY: State University of New York Press, 2007); and Russell Goodman, "William James," in *The Stanford Encyclopedia of Philosophy*, ed. Edward Zalta (2013), accessed February 9, 2016, http: //plato. stanford.edu/ entries/james/.

9. Henry James, ed., *The Letters of William James* (Boston: Little, Brown, & Co, 1926), 393–4.

MODULE 6
SECONDARY IDEAS

KEY POINTS

* *The Principles of Psychology* considers how we might formulate a psychological* understanding of our sense perceptions.
* Because he had access to only rudimentary knowledge about how we see and listen, James's analysis remains fragmentary.
* On inspection, several of James's offhand observations about the individual psyche reveal implicit insights.

Other Ideas

Besides the idea of "stream of consciousness,"* William James's *Principles of Psychology* also explores a number of other key themes. But we should note that calling "stream of consciousness" the primary theme imposes an artificial distinction James might not have accepted. Still, he raises a number of additional ideas worth exploring.

First, James discusses habits, instincts, and whether people make free choices or merely act on instinct. One scholar notes that "James did not believe that instinctive behavior" in humans "is blind and invariable," but rather it is behavior we are aware of, "modifiable by experience."[1] In other words, most people choose to sleep on a soft bed rather than the floor or to eat steak rather than dirt; experience has taught them to prefer comfort rather than austerity. In contrast, think of an experience we might consider "mindless": when I stand in a room, I always face the middle of it; I have done this many times before, and my brain has become accustomed to this activity.[2] The theme of internal and external remains important here: externally, when we enter a room we automatically face the middle of it (rather than the wall). Internally, we can alter this behavior by choosing to look at the wall each time we enter a room, generating an external reminder. We are not born with those preferences (for beds, steak, facing the middle of a room). They represent learned patterns of behavior. And that learning creates a neural pathway in the physical brain—literally changing the structure of our brain.

James examines emotions in a similar way. He sees emotions as not merely the internal reflections of external events, but as events resulting from the interplay of internal and external. An emotion does not exist merely as a mental state; it is a physical state: anger causes our heart to race, our face to flush, and our muscles to clench. So if I see a bear and get scared, the bear did not create that fear. Seeing the bear provokes a physical reaction, and that reaction causes me to become frightened.[3]

> "The great thing, then, in all education, is to make our nervous system our ally instead of our enemy. It is to fund and capitalize our acquisitions, and live at ease upon the interest of the fund. For this we must make automatic and habitual, as early as possible, as many useful actions as we can, and guard against the growing into ways that are likely to be disadvantageous to us, as we should guard against the plague."
>
> ——William James, *The Principles of Psychology*

Exploring the Ideas

In James's view, we mediate habit and emotion both externally and internally, and free will* plays a significant role in that process. Our consciousness and recall are selective and personal: we choose what we experience and how we interpret those events. James felt that habit "dooms us all to fight out the battle of life upon the lines of our nurture or our early choice, and to make the best of a pursuit that disagrees, because there is no other for which we are fitted, and it is too late to begin again."[4]

Habits are not necessarily destiny though: we can choose our habits and even alter them through force of will: if you eat healthy food from an early age, you will develop a habit of eating healthy food[5]—but if you eat unhealthily as a child, you can teach yourself to develop a habit of healthy eating later in life. So one's behaviors result from consciousness and body working in tandem.

One's emotions result from a similar interplay, and remain similarly subject to consciousness. "Whistling to keep up courage is no mere figure of speech," James observed.[6] One feels emotions as a result of physical feelings—an internal state resulting from an external (mental state becomes physical reality). But one can decide what one's mental state ought to be, and work to alter the physical reality—whistling instead of cowering—and thereby work on the mental state. This argument would become known as the "James–Lange" theory of emotion, after James and the Danish physician Carl Lange,* who formulated a similar theory.

For both actions and emotions, where we turn our attention

makes a difference. James held that the "effort of attention is thus the essential phenomenon of will."[7] Most of the time, humans remain creatures of habit, buffeted along precarved neural pathways by outside events. But through selectivity of consciousness and the effort to pay attention, we can achieve something approximating free will.

Overlooked

Of all the ideas William James presents in *The Principles of Psychology*, his discussion of the processes of sensation and perception has perhaps suffered from some minor neglect. In fact, researchers in the field have largely ignored James's contributions to these areas of inquiry; as one commentator remarks, "writers and researchers on the topics of sensation and perception rarely cite James's ideas or even terminology as seminal for their own work— by contrast with his still very much alive-and-well assertions about emotion."[8] This occurs despite the fact that James's chapters on sensation and perception "are filled with insights and examples both from 'real life' and from the laboratory." They can "at the very least ... help students and researchers locate their narrow, parochial problems,"that is, narrowly construed technical questions,"in a richer, broader psychological/philosophical context."[9]

Why have scholars largely overlooked James's ideas on sensation and perception? It cannot be blamed on a lack of discussion in the text. On the contrary, James actually "devoted several chapters to perceptual issues."[10] Despite his lengthy discussion of these topics, some have suggested that "it is hard to

see on the surface any more in James' treatment of sensation and
perception than intelligent and well-informed commentary."[11]

---

1. B. R. Hergenhahn, *An Introduction to the History of Psychology* (Belmont: Wadsworth, 2009), 342.
2. Hergenhahn, *Introduction*, 342.
3. Hergenhahn, *Introduction*, 344.
4. William James, *The Principles of Psychology*, *Vols 1–2* (Cambridge, MA: Harvard University Press, 1981), 121.
5. James, *Principles*, 11.
6. James, *Principles*, 576.
7. James, *Principles*, 317.
8. William N. Dember, "William James on Sensation and Perception," *Psychological Science* 1, no. 3 (1990): 163–6.
9. Dember, "William James," 166.
10. Dember, "William James," 164.
11. Dember, "William James," 166.

ACHIEVEMENT

KEY POINTS

* *The Principles of Psychology* helped a new science come into being. In order to do this, James analyzed themes from ancient philosophy to religious studies.

* The author's later published works and lectures, in particular *The Varieties of Religious Experience* and *The Will to Believe*, illuminate deeper patterns of thought begun in *The Principles of Psychology.*

* While scholars abandoned some of James's arguments fairly quickly, with the birth of cognitive science* in the 1960s (the science of the ways in which the mind processes information), researchers once again focused on the internal workings of human thought—territory James had investigated nearly three-quarters of a century before.

Assessing the Argument

In *The Principles of Psychology*, William James remains primarily concerned with bringing to light the foundational laws of the science of psychology.* Analyzing his observations in a unique and introspective* style, James demonstrated the essence and power of psychology. This becomes particularly clear in the work's exploration of individual experience.

In many ways, James remained somewhat uncomfortable with the contribution he made to psychology. "On the one hand," writes one commentator, James "brought the new experimental* psychology to the United States; by founding a psychology laboratory at Harvard in the 1870s." But he "was never comfortable with the new psychology and always maintained his intellectual distance from it."[1] Modern schools of psychology may claim him as an ancestor for his promotion of psychology as a science, but if James were alive, he might consider this a dubious achievement.

For one scholar,"psychology today is the type of psychology James outlined," in that it is "willing to embrace all aspects of human existence and to employ those techniques found to be effective."[2] That may be a fine argument, but it is not one James would have made. James wrote of his own masterwork,"No subject is worth being treated of in 1, 000 pages." James felt he had merely rambled on without focus, concluding "1st that there is no such thing as a science of psychology, and 2nd that [William James] is an incapable."[3]

> "William James was an original thinker in and between the disciplines of physiology,* psychology and philosophy. His twelve-hundred page masterwork, The Principles of Psychology (1890), is a rich blend of physiology, psychology, philosophy, and personal reflection that has given us such ideas as 'the stream of thought' and the baby's impression of the world 'as one great blooming, buzzing confusion' (p462). It contains [the] seeds of pragmatism* and phenomenology,* and influenced generations of thinkers in Europe and America, including Edmund Husserl,* Bertrand Russell,* John Dewey,* and Ludwig Wittgenstein.*"
>
> —— Russell Goodman,* "William James," The Stanford Encyclopedia of Philosophy

Achievement in Context

Exploring some of James's other works offers a deeper understanding of *The Principles of Psychology*. The other two works that added most to his fame remain his 1902 collection, *The Varieties of Religious Experience*, a series of lectures he delivered at the beginning of the twentieth century, and *The Will to Believe*, published in 1897. In both these works, James expanded on the discussion of religious experience begun in his earliest essays and continued in *The Principles of Psychology*.

Although James's previous work had made him well known, *Principles* gained him international recognition. He "professed disgust at the size of the work," however, with its intimidating length over two volumes, and revised it in 1892, producing the single volume *Psychology: Briefer Course*.[4] "Almost half of this work was rewritten or new material; for years it was the most popular English text in psychology, often called, because of its comparative brevity, the Jimmy course," a play on the diminutive form of James.[5]

Whether James presented his methods of introspection* and reflection on one's own inner processes in one volume or two, they quickly fell out of favor. Scholars replaced them with more analytical, laboratory-based methods. "The 'laboratory blackguards' [that is, villains], as James disparagingly called them, were taking psychology in a direction he was unwilling to follow," and he moved out of psychology and into more philosophical pursuits.[6]

Limitations

The Principles of Psychology profoundly influenced the establishment of psychology as a legitimate science. But some of James's ideas have had limited influence. James endorsed functionalism,* a school that essentially sought to understand the functional *purpose* of behavior and consciousness.[7] He offered functionalism as an alternative perspective to the structuralism* advocated by the German physician and philosopher Wilhelm Wundt* and the British psychologist Edward Tichener ("structuralism" here denoting an approach founded on the analysis of the elements that together form a system). But some— including his teacher Wundt—leapt to criticize James. One scholar writes of "Wundt the experimentalist who, after reading James's *Principles* commented, 'It is literature, it is beautiful, but it is not psychology.'"[8] "Experimentalism" refers to an approach to psychology in which laboratory experiment is key. While functionalism remained an important influence in psychology in America, the concerns about the unscientific nature of this perspective diminished its influence on psychology as a whole.

Critics also noted that James's method of introspection remained purely subjective in nature. Psychologists quickly began to explore more objective methods of studying the mind and behavior. Indeed, by the 1920s, behaviorism*—an approach in which psychological processes were determined through an analysis of behavior, which can be measured by observation— had already begun to become more prominent than James's functionalism. Many of James's ideas about the mind and mental processes gave way to a focus on overt (visible) behavior.

Some behaviorists remained quite comfortable with the idea that "behavior can be described and explained without making reference to mental events or to internal psychological processes."[9] But with the birth of cognitive science in the 1960s, a new generation of researchers sought to understand the mind and cognitive processes. Advances in technology allowed them to do so in systematic, reliable ways.

---

1. Edward S. Reed, *From Soul to Mind: The Emergence of Psychology from Erasmus Darwin to William James* (New Haven, CT: Yale University Press, 1997), 201.

2. B. R. Hergenhahn, *An Introduction to the History of Psychology* (Belmont: Wadsworth, 2009), 377.

3. William James, *The Principles of Psychology, Vols 1–2* (Cambridge, MA: Harvard University Press, 1981), 294.

4. William James, *Psychology: Briefer Course* (Cambridge, MA, and London: Harvard University Press, 1984).

5. Gerald E. Myers, "Introduction: The Intellectual Context," in *Principles of Psychology*, XXXVI.

6. Rand B. Evans, "Introduction: The Historical Context," in *Principles of Psychology*, XI.

7. Kendra Cherry, "Structuralism and Functionalism: Early Schools of Thought in Psychology," *About. com*, accessed January 17, 2016, http: //psychology. about.com/od/historyofpsychology/a/structuralism.htm.

8. B. R. Hergenhahn and Tracy B. Henley, *An Introduction to the History of Psychology* (Belmont: Wadsworth, 2013), 326.

9. George Graham, "Behaviorism," *Stanford Encyclopedia of Philosophy*, accessed January 17, 2016, http: //plato.stanford.edu/archives/sum2012/entries/behaviorism/.

MODULE 8
PLACE IN THE AUTHOR'S WORK

KEY POINTS

* Throughout his work, James primarily concerned himself with the mystery of the inner life of a person and its physical, external signs.

* James's body of work does not contain a unifying theme; his works all contain examples from everyday life that illustrate his theories.

* Although not his first or last great success, *The Principles of Psychology* remains the keystone of James's legacy and cemented his reputation as the "founding father of psychology."*

Positioning

By the time *The Principles of Psychology* was published in 1890, William James had already begun to establish himself as a leading proponent of psychology and a foundational figure in its establishment as a science. His interest in psychology became clear as early as 1878, when he published the essay "Remarks on Spencer's Definition of Mind as Correspondence."[1] The following year saw another essay, "The Sentiment of Rationality" (reprinted in *The Will to Believe and Other Essays in Popular Philosophy*),[2] which he revised and republished in 1882. Both works significantly foreshadow *The Principles of Psychology* in a variety of ways.

But James wrote the works most explicitly tied to the thoughts in *Principles* after his masterwork. These include *The Will to Believe*, originally published in 1897; *The Varieties of Religious*

Experience,[3] published in 1902, and James's flurry of late writings: *Pragmatism*,[4] *A Pluralistic Universe*,[5] and *Essays in Radical Empiricism*,[6] published in 1907, 1909, and 1912, respectively.

We may find undeniable patterns and repetitions of thinking throughout James's publications, but the centerpiece of his intellectual explorations—his lifelong search for the foundational laws of psychology—does not appear in all his works. We may find some value in considering *The Principles of Psychology* as a prism through which we can view the author's earlier and later works, but many of James's works, including *The Principles of Psychology*, lack a lucid center of thought. This poses a significant challenge to scholars trying to make a coherent case for his body of work. As some scholars have suggested, James's book remains uniquely important because it offers singularly profound insights into the nature of uncertainty.

> "William James's thought epitomizes the ambivalent bonding between philosophy and psychology."
>
> ——Gerald E. Myers, Introduction to William James, *The Principles of Psychology*

Integration

We cannot consider James's body of work to be coherent and unified. Although significant themes do recur in each of his works. Some are included accidentally, as when James resists Wilhelm Wundt's* claim that every intentional act contains a singular, unique sense—what is called a "feeling of innervation."*

In *Principles* and throughout his other works, James penetrates the layers of everyday moments to illustrate his theories—unsystematically, perhaps, but not at the cost of any valuable insight: "I sit at table after dinner and find myself from time to time taking nuts or raisins out of the dish and eating them. My dinner properly is over, and in the heat of the conversation I am hardly aware of what I do; but the perception of the fruit, and the fleeting notion that I may eat it, seem fatally to bring the act about. There is certainly no express fiat [that is, order or requirement] here."[7]

Significance

Scholars often refer to James as the father of American psychology—an honor placing him in the remarkable ranks of other scientific "founding fathers" such as Jean-Martin Charcot* (a pioneer in the field of neurology*—the science of the brain and nervous system) and Sigmund Freud* (the founder of psychoanalysis*—a therapeutic and theoretical approach to the unconscious mind). Like them, James makes a strong case for his discipline as a modern science. *The Principles of Psychology* offers unique insight into the internal and external dynamic of psychic phenomena. Moreover, James's explorations of experience enhance our understanding of insight—he transforms our very thinking about how we acquire it.

James's innovations opened up wholly new opportunities for psychology to inform nonpsychological activities. Instead of analyzing thought as if it were a static series of images, psychologists—indeed, people from outside strictly scientific fields altogether, including artists—could now think of (and even celebrate) experience as a ceaselessly flowing stream of consciousness.*

As a philosopher, William James enjoys the status of a canonical figure: "William James," writes one commentator, "is to classic American philosophy as Plato* was to Greek and Roman philosophy, as an originating and inspirational fountainhead."[8] James's work proved to be defining in its areas of concern, such as the stream of consciousness or the concept of the mind itself as activity. But his approach—pragmatism*—also redefined the discipline. Pragmatism remains a distinctively American approach to philosophy. Rejecting the lofty concerns of his European contemporaries, James approached such questions as "Is there a soul?" in terms of their practical value: does the answer tell us something realistic and distinctive in the simplest possible way? For these reasons James's body of work, especially *Principles*, has enjoyed sustained acclaim.

1. William James, "Remarks on Spencer's Definition of Mind as Correspondence," *Journal of Speculative Philosophy* 12, no. 1 (1878): 1–18.
2. William James, *The Will to Believe and Other Essays in Popular Philosophy* (Cambridge, MA, and London: Harvard University Press, 1979).
3. William James, *The Varieties of Religious Experience* (New York: Barnes and Noble, 2004).
4. William James, *Pragmatism* (New York: Dover Publications, 1907).
5. William James, *A Pluralistic Universe* (Cambridge, MA: Harvard University Press, 1909).
6. William James, *Essays in Radical Empiricism* (London: Longmans, Green and Co, 1912).
7. William James, *The Principles of Psychology*, Vols 1–2 (Cambridge, MA: Harvard University Press, 1981), 1131.
8. John McDermott, quoted in Richard D. Richardson Jr., *William James: In the Maelstrom of American Modernism: A Biography* (Boston: Mariner, 2006), xiv.

SECTION 3
IMPACT

THE FIRST RESPONSES

KEY POINTS

* Although it received mixed reviews, critics never mounted a concerted rejection of *The Principles of Psychology.*

* The "father of psychology"* drifted away from psychology as his contemporaries grew more pretentious, he believed, about their newly recognized science.

* James set the stage for what would become known as the functionalist* school; later scientists fleshed out its principles more fully.

Criticism

The mixed reception given to William James's *The Principles of Psychology* is perhaps understandable given the range of subjects it examines without a central thesis on which to hang them. Typical responses praised individual parts of the book, such as James's treatment of the "stream of consciousness,"* but generally took issue with its extensive use of the introspective method—self-examination is not perhaps the most conducive means to arrive at any objective (impartial, disinterested) analysis. The philosopher C. S. Peirce,* for example, wrote that James's introspective method amounts to "the uncritical acceptance of data ... which would make a complete rupture with accepted methods of psychology and of science in general."[1]

In general, critics held that, while *Principles* may be insightful, beautiful, profound, and philosophical, it clashed with the increasingly fashionable tendency to treat psychology as a "hard" science like biology. The Spanish philosopher George Santayana* remained skeptical of James's attribution of material causes to psychological effects. Referencing "materialists,"* those scientists for whom all phenomena should be explained by physical causes, he wrote that James had "outdone the materialists themselves," applying "the principle of the total and immediate dependence of mind on matter to several fields in which we are still accustomed only to metaphysical* or psychological hypotheses"[2] ("metaphysics" refers to the branch of philosophy dealing with the most fundamental questions of existence and knowledge).

> *"Fortunately for William James, American psychology, philosophy, and American letters in general, his estimations of himself, his book, and its future were grossly in error. For American psychology James's* Principles *represents the point of demarcation between the traditional philosophical psychologies and the new experimental psychologies."*
>
> —— Rand B. Evans, "Introduction: The Historical Context," in William James, *The Principles of Psychology*

Responses

Responding to one critic, James defended himself using some strong language. He said he had chosen to write unsystematically "on account of the strong aversion with which I am filled for the humbugging pretense of exactitude in the way of definition of terms and description of states that has prevailed in psychological

literature."[3] Ultimately James largely abandoned experimental*
psychology, the scientific pretensions of his colleagues having
driven him away. He found the discipline had increasingly become
what he considered a "hair splitting" physical science, characterized
by rapid empirical* development rather than reflection and
invention. Although he republished *Principles* in 1892 as the
shorter work that became popularly known as the "Jimmy" course,[4]
he never revised his core arguments about the connections between
mind and body or consciousness being understandable as some
kind of stream.

He responded to critics more fully with one of his last works
in psychology, *The Physical Basis of Emotion*,[5] in which he
restated the case that simple sensations like pleasure and pain were
not transmitted by special nerves (as reductionists* might argue)
but resulted from the interaction of mental states and physical
stimuli.

Conflict and Consensus

James set the tone for much of what would become the functionalist
school of thought (according to which, given the demands of
our evolutionary history, mental states must serve some kind of
function). But the school would not come into its own until later
in the twentieth century, when the influential psychologists John
Dewey* and James Angell* "stressed the functional significance
of adaptive behavior and viewed mind as mediating between
the environment and the needs of the organism."[6] This way of
thinking moved past introspection* as a methodology. These new

functionalists studied only what could be observed.

Many early behaviorists* (for whom psychological research could only be conducted through what was observable, i.e. behavior) began their academic careers as functionalists. One scholar notes that some "were impressed by how much could be learned about humans without the use of introspection, and they began to drift toward what was later called the behavioristic position."[7] As the functionalist psychologist James Cattell* wrote,"The time of mental processes, the accuracy of perception and movement, the range of consciousness, fatigue and practise, the motor accompaniments of thought, memory, the association of ideas, the perception of space," were able to be analyzed with purely experimental, observational methods. "I have investigated [these phenomena] without requiring the slightest introspection on the part of the subject or undertaking such on my own part during the course of the experiments."[8] In other words, Cattell dismissed introspection as unscientific and unworthy of psychology-as-science.

---

1. C. S. Peirce, *Writings of Charles S. Peirce: A Chronological Edition*, *Volume 8: 1890–1892* (Peirce Edition Project, 2010), 234.

2. George Santayana, quoted in Gerald E. Myers, "Introduction: The Intellectual Context," in William James, *The Principles of Psychology*, *Vols 1–2* (Cambridge, MA: Harvard University Press, 1981), XXXVII-XXXVIII.

3. Michael M. Sokal, Introduction to William James, *Psychology: Briefer Course* (Cambridge, MA, and London: Harvard University Press, 1984), XXXVIII.

4. James, *Psychology: Briefer Course*.

5. William James, "The Physical Basis of Emotion," *Psychological Review* 101, no. 2 (1994): 205–10.

6. O. L. Zangwill, in *The Oxford Companion to Mind*, ed. Richard L. Gregory, accessed February 8, 2016, http://ezproxy-prd.bodleian.ox.ac.uk: 2232/view/10.1093/acref/9780198662242.001.0001/acref-9780198662242-e-356?rskey=xS72i4&result=1.

7. B. R. Hergenhahn, *An Introduction to the History of Psychology* (Belmont: Wadsworth, 2009), 384.

8. Hergenhahn, *Introduction*, 384.

MODULE 10
THE EVOLVING DEBATE

KEY POINTS

- James's writing attracted many followers; the fields of phenomenology* (inquiry into issues regarding perception and knowledge) and Gestalt psychology* (a school of thought that examines the mind and body as a whole, rather than treating them as separate components) both owe something to James's innovations.

- While never inspiring a cohesive school of thought, James's insights remain inspirational.

- Modern thinkers who have benefited from James's work include the twentieth-century Austrian British philosopher of language Ludwig Wittgenstein.*

Uses and Problems

In *The Principles of Psychology*, William James articulated a functionalist* approach, considering psychological* phenomena to be serving some function vital to the human organism in the light of our evolutionary history. The approach initiated a debate with those of the structuralist* school, for whom the mind could (and should) only be considered as a system made up of integrated components such as reactions and sensations. The debate continued until functionalist principles were widely adopted in the field.

Functionalism is related to the phenomenology associated with the psychologist-philosopher Edmund Husserl,* another scholar influenced by James. While some schools saw mental events as merely elements, phenomenology saw them as entire events rather than the sums of parts.

Husserl wanted to describe the pure experience of, say, seeing an apple in all its facets. Adherents of other schools of thought would break the experience down into parts—perceiving "redness," "roundness," its quality as a fruit, and so on. Phenomenology sees perception as a whole experience. Rather than asking what someone perceives, one must first know what the holistic experience of perceiving something is—we do not, after all, judge a symphony by its individual notes but by the overall impressions it inspires.

Practitioners of Gestalt psychology, who may be seen as descendants of Husserl, took James's concept of a stream of consciousness* further; they argued that we may study the mind in terms of its elements, but only with the understanding that those elements consisted of whole thoughts—thus the name "Gestalt," German for "whole."

Critics of Gestalt psychology often sounded a lot like the earlier critics of James's work. They called Gestalt psychology imprecise and subjective (Gestaltists would see this as a strength). Eventually the theory became folded into other schools of psychology* (especially alternatives to the mainstream schools of psychoanalysis* and behaviorism,* such as cognitive science).*

"This work proceeds by a series of experiments, by means of which we have learned to live (for the most part) without 'polygamy and slavery, private warfare and liberty to kill, judicial torture and arbitrary royal power.'"*

—Russell Goodman on William James's *The Will to Believe*

Schools of Thought

The American philosopher John Dewey* distilled functionalism into a coherent school of thought. In his formulation, it was characterized by a belief that the elements of psychology serve a given function dictated by evolution. In other words, consciousness helps people decide between complex options. Dewey applied James's principle of the "stream of consciousness" to actions, which we may think of as the "stream of behaviors." While other thinkers divided actions into different parts (stimuli and responses), Dewey did not. He offered the example of a child reaching out to touch a candle flame, and then withdrawing his hand from the heat: "The experience of being burned," Dewey noted, "changes the child's perception of the flame."[1] This happens only as "the child was still observing the flame while being burned and withdrew ... the so-called stimuli and responses are not separate but form an interrelated sequence of functional events," and the future stimulus imparted by the candle flame will no longer be attraction, but avoidance.[2]

Functionalism was taken further—and into the laboratory—by the psychologist E. L. Thorndike,* one of James's students, who derived the laws of effect and exercise. The law of effect states that of several possible responses to a given stimulus the ones that accord most with the animal's will are most likely to recur, while those in opposition to the animal's will be least likely. The law of exercise states that any response to a situation will become more strongly connected to that situation as it occurs more often and with greater intensity.[3] Ultimately, scientists incorporated functionalism's main insights into the wider study of psychology. This occurred largely because of its pragmatic approach and its assumption that behaviors perform evolutionary functions.

In Current Scholarship

The twentieth-century Austrian British philosopher Ludwig Wittgenstein is one of James's key intellectual descendants. Wittgenstein was attracted to James's pragmatism* more than to his discussion of the mind and consciousness. *Principles* offered Wittgenstein "a pragmatist philosophical persona; nonfanatical, concerned to avoid the grip of theory, attuned to the human interests served by our theorizing, and flexible enough to move on without having every question answered."[4]

Wittgenstein's highly influential 1953 work, *Philosophical Investigations*, aimed to uncover the principles of language. Wittgenstein believed that language—not just "words," but also the very ideas of meaning in general—becomes conditioned by experience.[5] Take the saying,"Thank my lucky stars." Said by someone from ancient Rome, it expresses genuine gratitude for a divine entity the man believes has intervened in some way. But a modern person uses the same words as a mere figure of speech, expressing relief.

So in Wittgenstein's view, language has no universal rules, nor can we understand it by breaking it down into its parts. We must understand it in context, and recognize that different contexts produce different meanings. When someone standing in a library says: "Look at my family tree," he likely means a document describing his genealogy. But if someone standing in a field said the same thing, he is likely referring to an actual tree standing on his family's property.

---

1. B. R. Hergenhahn, *Introduction to the History of Psychology* (Belmont: Wadsworth, 2009), 363.

2. Hergenhahn, *Introduction*, 363.

3. Hergenhahn, *Introduction*, 342–3.

4. Russell Goodman, *Wittgenstein and William James* (Cambridge: Cambridge University Press, 2002), 19.

5. Ludwig Wittgenstein, *Philosophical Investigations*, trans. P. M. S. Hacker and Joachim Schulte (Chichester: John Wiley and Sons, 2009).

IMPACT AND INFLUENCE TODAY

KEY POINTS

* *The Principles of Psychology* remains a key work in the history of the science of psychology* after more than a century.

* Behaviorists* have continued to feed off James's functionalist* ideas, and still do so today.

* Today, science devotes much attention to questions of artificial intelligence; cognitive scientists* extend James's work by debating the definition of "consciousness"—and of who or what can display it.

Position

William James's *Principles of Psychology* remains a key work in the history of psychology and philosophy even if it no longer plays a major role in modern debate. The discipline has largely moved on from James's methodology of introspection* to formal logic, neuroscience (the science of the nervous system and the brain) or controlled experiments. However, because of this subjectivity— that is, the fact that its findings are fundamentally influenced by the experience of the author—it remains a key work in the history of both psychology and philosophy "that no longer occurs in psychology textbooks."[1]

References to *Principles* throughout the twentieth century may be rather cosmetic,"In mainstream experimental* psychology, references to James during [the latter half of the twentieth century] typically take the form of a historic salute rather than being a serious consideration of James's ideas."[2] However, the prominent US psychologist Gordon Allport* felt we could learn a few fundamental lessons from *Principles*: "Narrow consistency can neither bring salvation to your science, nor help to mankind. Let your approaches be diverse ... If you find yourselves tangled in paradoxes, what of that?"[3] In other words, James's enduring message has been to recommend that psychologists and philosophers be pragmatic in their study, and not restrict themselves unduly to one approach if doing so compromises analytical usefulness.

> "Habit is thus the enormous fly-wheel of society, its most precious conservative agent. It alone is what keeps us all within the bounds of ordinance, and saves the children of fortune from the envious uprisings of the poor."
>
> —— William James, *The Principles of Psychology*

Interaction

The behaviorist school of thought continues to respond to the concerns of James and his descendants. For behaviorists, psychology should concern itself with observable actions rather than the mental state or the thought. The twentieth-century psychologist B. F. Skinner* took behaviorism one step further, founding a school known as "radical behaviorism." Skinner called "introspection" a fuzzy process, believing that people used mental terms like "satisfaction," "choosing," and so on, as a best-guess approximation of neurological* events actually happening in their brains. Skinner wrote,"A completely independent science of subjective experience would have no more bearing on a science of behavior than a science of what people feel about fire would have on the science of combustion."[4]

Unlike the investigation of mental states, which must be interpreted and reported, behaviorism assumes that scientists can only measure behavior and the external stimuli that determine it. As the behaviorist John Watson* explained,"given the stimulus, psychology can predict what the response will be; or, on the other hand, given the response, it can specify the nature of the effective stimulus."[5] This stimulus could be complex, such as a general environmental condition—a room perceived to be full of unfriendly people, for example, or something as simple as a ringing bell.

A number of scholars argue that some ideas in behaviorism have become central to psychology, just as the discipline adopted some functionalist ideas. As one wrote, "All modern psychologists restrict their evidence to observable behavior, attempt to specify stimuli and responses with the greatest possible precision, [and] are skeptical of theories that resist empirical* testing."[6] But the definition of what "evidence" is remains loose; many cognitive scientists* are looking at mental processes that are difficult to observe but that can be conceptualized through thought experiments (methods of exploring a hypothesis by a thorough consideration of its consequences).

The Continuing Debate

While James's work endures more as a historical artifact than as an

130

active player in psychological inquiry, it does inspire some current scholarship, particularly in the discipline of cognitive science, which aims to improve our understanding of consciousness. And although the discipline has not reached a consensus about what exactly constitutes consciousness, cognitive scientists continue to examine it on the basis of its"neurological and computational elements."[7] One of the key questions of cognitive psychology remains distinguishing "human" cognition (which is conscious) from artificial intelligence, which is not.

The pioneering British computer scientist Alan Turing* proposed a test to distinguish between intelligence (consciousness) and artificial intelligence (nonconsciousness). In it, a person sits at a computer, typing in a chat program, talking to a human or to a computer; if the computer succeeds at convincing the person that it is human, it can be considered conscious.

One of the ways this idea can be demonstrated is through the use of the philosopher John Searle's* idea of the "Chinese Room." This experiment involves the thinker imagining being seated in a room with a codebook and a number of symbols in a language they do not speak (for the purposes of the experiment, Chinese). The codebook indicates which symbols match up with other symbols. Someone slips in a question—written in the code language—and the thinker uses the book to assemble an answer. Although it is possible for a non-Chinese speaker to generate a perfect answer from a sufficiently well-written codebook, we cannot claim that the person performing the exercise "understands" Chinese. The mere ability to manipulate symbols does not guarantee cognition, perception, understanding, or thought. For computers that work by manipulating symbols, the simple ability to run the computer program does not guarantee cognition.[8] Searle argues that cognition depends on mental content: our brains give rise to consciousness (thinking about thinking, the act of understanding). This remains a higher-level activity than mere processing.[9]

---

1. Gerald E. Myers, "Introduction: The Intellectual Context," in William James, *The Principles of Psychology, Vols 1–2* (Cambridge, MA: Harvard University Press, 1981), XIV.

2. Myers, "Introduction," LXV.

3. Gordon Allport, "The Productive Paradoxes of William James," *Psychological Review* 50, no. 1 (1943): 95.

4. B. F. Skinner, quoted in B. R. Hergenhahn, *An Introduction to the History of Psychology* (Belmont: Wadsworth, 2009), 445.

5. John Watson, quoted in John A. Mills, *Control: A History of Behavioral Psychology* (New York: New York University Press), 9.

6. Bernard Baars, quoted in Hergenhahn, *Introduction*, 412.

7. Hergenhahn, *Introduction*, 634.

8. See Searle, quoted in Hergenhahn, *Introduction*, 630.

9. Searle, quoted in Hergenhahn, *Introduction*, 630.

MODULE 12
WHERE NEXT?

KEY POINTS

* Although James had no access to advanced technology when he wrote *The Principles of Psychology*, modern science has enabled researchers to verify and build on many of his insights.
* James's most enduring contribution may be his concept of the "stream of consciousness,"* which has been taken up by artists, scientists, and the general public alike.
* *Principles of Psychology* not only helped to inaugurate psychology* as a hard science, but also introduced several key concepts such as the physical basis of emotion.

Potential

In its time, William James's *The Principles of Psychology* did much to advance the conversation about how the brain developed and works. Twenty-first-century technology gives scientists much more sophisticated research tools. But their conclusions track quite well with some of James's insights, especially about the brain's structure and function.

Some of these insights suggest that James's analysis, unaided by technology, was remarkably accurate. In his paper "The Neurobiology of Learning and Memory: William James in Retrospect," Richard Thompson* argues that James's work anticipated modern scientific discoveries. Thompson notes that James "expressed ideas about brain localization* and plasticity in neural networks* that foreshadowed many aspects of current neurobiology."*[1] Scientists have discovered that certain parts of the brain handle certain functions—they call this concept "localization." These functions range from language to rational thought to visual sensation. Neuroplasticity—the idea that the brain creates neural pathways in response to experiences—relates somewhat to James's work on habit; James believed that habits can be altered by creating stronger habits.

> "By the 'spiritual me,' so far as it belongs to the empirical* self, I mean no one of my passing states of consciousness. I mean rather the entire collection of my states of consciousness, my psychic faculties and dispositions taken concretely. This collection can at any moment become an object to my thought at that moment and awaken emotions like those awakened by any of the other portions of the Me."
>
> —— William James, *The Principles of Psychology*

Future Directions

The core concerns James examined have helped to define some of the core questions psychologists continue to study. These questions include "What is a thought?", "What is consciousness?", and "Is there a relationship between 'mind' and 'body'?" But inn many ways the discipline of psychology concerns itself with metaphorical explanations such as the "stream of consciousness"—James's most enduring metaphor.

The idea of the stream of consciousness remains accessible even to laypeople, and it has served as a continual source of creativity. As one scholar noted, "The effort among artists to represent the stream of consciousness," through writing, film, and even painting,"provides us with a touchstone for our own experience."[2] However, it is more than just a narrative metaphor. Serious scholars still study it, investigating daydreaming, fantasizing, and "ongoing imaginative processes" through a stream of *creative* consciousness. Modern researchers go beyond the information James had access to by attempting to localize the stream of consciousness in hemispheres of the brain. They also investigate ways in which the stream of consciousness can liberate people from the workaday world of the senses.

Summary

William James saw psychology as a way to redeem the threatening meaninglessness of existence in modern time. "The social affections, all the various forms of play, the thrilling intimations of art, the delights of philosophic contemplation, the rest of religious emotion, the joy of moral self-approbation, the charm of fancy and of wit—some or all of these are absolutely required to make the notion of mere existence tolerable."[3] That desire to make existence "tolerable" drove his quest to establish psychology as a science. But these are not the words of a happy or contented man.

The Principles of Psychology revolutionized the discipline of psychology. James effectively distinguished it from philosophy without resorting to structuralism,* as his colleagues in Europe had. He also introduced several concepts still used today. He argued, for example, that emotions were not merely transmitted from the mind to the body. He held that the relationship went two ways (perceiving a monster makes you shiver, which makes you feel fear). His most important concept, however, was the "stream of consciousness," a view that holds that thought is not separable into its component parts, but rather is a constantly flowing stream of impressions and mental states. Beyond revolutionizing psychology, this also provided inspiration for some of the twentieth century's most celebrated works of literature.

James believed that we "satisfy at all times as many demands as we can." He saw this as proof that we are all striving towards a "richer universe ... the good which seems most organizable, most fit to enter into complex combinations, most apt to be a member of a more inclusive whole."[4]

1. Richard Thompson, "The Neurobiology of Learning and Memory: William James in Retrospect," *Psychological Science* 1, no. 3 (1990): 172.

2. Kenneth S. Pope and Jerome L. Singer, "Introduction: The Flow of Human Experience," in *The Stream of Consciousness*, ed. Kenneth S. Pope and Jerome L. Singer (New York: Springer, 1978), 3.

3. William James, *Essays in Philosophy* (Cambridge, MA, and London: Harvard University Press, 1978), 13.

4. William James, *The Will to Believe and Other Essays in Popular Philosophy* (Cambridge, MA, and London: Harvard University Press, 1979), 205, 210.

GLOSSARY OF TERMS

1. **Amazon River:** flowing through South America, the Amazon is one of the two longest rivers in the world. Many civilizations have flourished in the Amazon basin, parts of which to this day remain incredibly difficult to access.

2. **Behaviorism:** an approach to psychology founded on the notion that the mind can only be understood through observable behavior. Scientists, including B. F. Skinner, developed behaviorism in the early twentieth century.

3. **Capitalism:** an economic system, dominant in the West, in which privately owned companies operating in competitive markets pay wages to their workers for labor for the sake of private profit.

4. **Cognitive science:** an interdisciplinary field of science that examines how the mind processes information.

5. **Determinism:** the belief that our actions are determined by natural laws.

6. **Empirical:** verifiable by observation.

7. **Epiphenomenalism:** the belief that stimuli, such as external events or internal phenomena such as muscle contractions, cause mental events (thoughts or feelings).

8. **Experimentalism:** reliance on the use of controlled laboratory tests to establish proof in science.

9. **Free will:** the notion that human beings have the freedom to make choices that are not predetermined by external causes or divine intervention.

10. **Functionalism:** an approach to the sciences founded on the assumption that phenomena serve a vital function in the continuing operations of a system or organism; in psychology, functionalist approaches consider mental processes to be connected to biological imperatives or as reflecting the evolutionary history of our species.

11. **Gestalt psychology:** a school of thought that examines the mind and body as a whole, rather than treating them as separate components.

12. **Industrialization:** the process that moved large parts of the Western world from an agrarian, village-based economy to a manufacturing economy based

largely in cities. This process began in Britain in the early nineteenth century.

13. **Innervation:** literally, the act of supplying a muscle with nerves.

14. **Introspection:** from the Latin meaning *to look inward at*: an analysis of one's own emotion and mental process.

15. **Localization:** in neurobiology, this refers to the scientific effort to determine which regions of the brain engage with which emotions or actions.

16. **Materialists:** scientists and philosophers for whom physical matter is the foundation of everything we experience, including mental phenomena.

17. **Metaphysical:** relating to a branch of philosophy whose roots trace back to the ancient Greek philosopher Aristotle dealing with fundamental questions of existence and knowledge.

18. **Modernism:** a movement in European art, with its heyday in the early twentieth century, which challenged traditional forms and techniques.

19. **Nativism:** in psychology, the concept that we are born with certain skills and abilities already programmed into our brains.

20. **Neural network:** also known as a "neural pathway," a channel formed in the brain as a person has experiences or feels emotions.

21. **Neurology:** a branch of medicine dealing with the functioning of the nervous system.

22. **Phenomenology:** a school of philosophy founded in the early twentieth century by the German philosopher Edmund Husserl. Phenomenologists study consciousness and the phenomena associated with conscious acts.

23. **Physiology:** the study of the nature and functioning of organisms and their organs.

24. **Polygamy:** the practice of taking more than one spouse. While some societies and religions continue to practice polygamy, it has been outlawed in much of the developed world.

25. **Pragmatism:** a philosophical movement begun in the United States around

1870. Pragmatism holds that thoughts can best be used to predict, problem-solve, and act.

26. **Psychoanalysis:** a series of processes and techniques formulated around 1890 by the Austrian neurologist Sigmund Freud. It attempts to identify unconscious mental processes as a way to treat and cure mental disorders.

27. **Psychology:** the study of the mind and behavior.

28. **Reductionism:** the belief that a whole can be understood with reference to its component parts. Often, but not always, used pejoratively to discuss approaches to complex problems that do not take into account "the big picture."

29. **Renaissance:** a period in European cultural history, usually understood as the fourteenth to sixteenth centuries, in which artists turned towards ancient Roman and Greek models to reinvigorate European culture.

30. **Second Industrial Revolution:** an expansion of industrialization, begun around 1870 when electric-powered machines enabled production to become further automated.

31. **Stream of consciousness:** a concept pioneered by William James that relates to the flow of thoughts in the conscious (and unconscious) mind.

32. **Structuralism:** a school of thought that arose at the beginning of the twentieth century that seeks to look at entities as a whole, rather than at their component parts.

33. **Swedenborgism:** a Christian religious movement founded in England in 1787 that takes its beliefs from the writings of the Swedish scientist and theologian Emanuel Swedenborg.

34. **Uprootedness:** the sense of being removed from all that is familiar geographically, physically, and culturally.

1. **Jean Louis Agassiz (1807–73)** was a Swiss biologist and geologist, whose many contributions to natural science have been clouded by the fact that he rejected Darwinism.

2. **Gordon Allport (1897–1967)** was an American psychologist who rejected psychiatry and behaviorism and focused on the individual as a unique person ("personality psychology").

3. **James Angell (1869–1949)** was an American psychologist known for his work at Yale University and a key figure in functionalism (in psychology, the belief that mental processes are founded in biological imperatives).

4. **Aristotle (384–322 B.C.E.)** was a student of Plato who became one of the foremost philosophers of Ancient Greece. His entry in the *Encyclopedia Britannica* calls him "the first genuine scientist in history."

5. **James Cattell (1860–1944)** was an American psychologist; the first professor of psychology in the US, he helped establish it as a legitimate science.

6. **Jean-Martin Charcot (1825–93)** was a French neurologist, often considered the father of modern neurology.

7. **Charles Darwin (1809–82)** was an English naturalist and geologist, famous for his theory of evolution set out in his 1859 work, *On the Origin of Species*.

8. **René Descartes (1596–1650)** was a French philosopher, mathematician, and scientist. He is considered by many to be the father of Western philosophy, and is best remembered for the statement "*cogito, ergo sum*" ("I think therefore I am").

9. **John Dewey (1859–1952)** was an American philosopher, psychologist, and educational reformer. Scholars consider him one of the founders of functional psychology.

10. **Sigmund Freud (1856–1939)** was an Austrian neurologist considered the father of the therapeutic and theoretical approach to the unconscious mind known as psychoanalysis.

11. **Russell Goodman** is a popular, academic authority on William James, based at the University of New Mexico.

12. **Hermann von Helmholtz (1821–94)** was a German physician who is remembered for his work on human sensory systems.

13. **Shadworth Holloway Hodgson (1832–1912)** was an English philosopher. James acknowledged him as the founder of pragmatism.

14. **David Hume (1711–76)** was a Scottish philosopher, historian, and economist known for his impact on empiricism, naturalism, and skepticism.

15. **Edmund Husserl (1859–1938)** was a German philosopher who established the school of phenomenology.

16. **Henry James (1843–1916)** was the younger brother of William. A novelist and literary critic, he spent much of his life in England, and many of his works—*The Wings of the Dove* (1902) and *The Golden Bowl* (1904) among them—deal with the contrast between the European and American character.

17. **James Joyce (1882–1941)** was an Irish novelist and poet known for his influential modernist literary style.

18. **Immanuel Kant (1724–1804)** was a German philosopher who is generally recognized as a central figure of modern philosophy. His work inspired many subsequent generations of philosophers around the world.

19. **Carl Lange (1834–1900)** was a Danish physician who made significant contributions to neurology, psychiatry, and psychology.

20. **John Locke (1632–1704)** was an English physician and an empiricist philosopher. He formulated a "theory of mind" that gave rise to the modern concepts of identity and the self.

21. **C. S. Peirce (1839–1914)** was an American philosopher. He made significant contributions to a number of fields but is most famous as a logician and the founder of pragmatism.

22. **Plato (c. 427–348 B.C.E.)** was one of the foremost philosophers of the ancient world; his work laid the foundation for studies in science and Western philosophy.

23. **Marcel Proust (1871–1922)** was a French novelist and critic best known for

his seven-volume novel *À la recherche du temps perdu* (*Remembrance of Things Past*).

24. **Bertrand Russell (1872–1970)** was a British philosopher and political activist, who joined with his protégé Ludwig Wittgenstein and others to found the school of analytic philosophy.

25. **George Santayana (1863–1952)** was a Spanish-born philosopher, writer of poetry, novels, and essays, and a cultural critic.

26. **John Searle (b. 1932)** is an American philosopher and academic, most famous for his work on the philosophy of language and the philosophy of mind.

27. **B. F. Skinner (1904–90)** was an American psychologist and one of the leading figures in the radical behaviorism school.

28. **Richard Thompson (1930–2014)** was one of the world's leading neuroscientists. He did groundbreaking work on the science of learning and memory.

29. **E. L. Thorndike (1874–1949)** was an American psychologist who focused on comparative psychology and how people learn.

30. **Alan Turing (1912–54)** was a pioneering British computer scientist, most famous to the general public for having cracked the German's "Enigma code" during World War II. Scholars consider him to be the father of artificial intelligence.

31. **John Watson (1878–1958)** was an American psychologist and founder of the behaviorist school.

32. **Ludwig Wittgenstein (1889–1951)** was an Austrian British philosopher who worked mostly in logic, the philosophy of the mind, and language. Although he published very little in his lifetime, his posthumous collection, *Philosophical Investigations*, remains one of the most important philosophical works of the twentieth century.

33. **Virginia Woolf (1882–1941)** was an English writer of novels, essays, and criticism and a leading literary modernist.

34. **Wilhelm Wundt (1832–1920)** was a German physician, philosopher, and psychologist, the first to distinguish psychology from biology and philosophy.

 **WORKS CITED**

1. Allport, Gordon. "The productive paradoxes of William James." *Psychological Review* 50, no. 1 (1943): 95–120.

2. Buss, David. *Evolutionary Psychology: The New Science of the Mind.* Boston: Pearson, 2008.

3. Cherry, Kendra. "Structuralism and Functionalism: Early Schools of Thought in Psychology." *About. com.* Accessed February 8, 2016. http://psychology.about.com/od/historyofpsychology/a/structuralism.htm.

4. Darwin, Charles. *The Origin of Species.* New York: P. F. Collier and Son, 1909.

5. Dember, William N. "William James on Sensation and Perception." *Psychological Science* 1, no. 3 (1990): 163–6.

6. Gavin, William J. *William James in Focus: Willing to Believe.* Bloomington: Indiana University Press, 2013.

7. Goodman, Russell. "William James." *Stanford Encyclopedia of Philosophy*, edited by Edward Zalta, 2013. Accessed February 10, 2016. http: //plato.stanford.edu/entries/james/.

8. Graham, George. "Behaviorism." *Stanford Encyclopedia of Philosophy, edited by Edward Zalta*, 2012. Accessed February 8, 2016. http://plato.stanford.edu/archives/sum2012/entries/behaviorism/.

9. Hawkins, Stephanie L. "William James, Gustav Fechner, and Early Psychophysics." *Frontiers in Physiology* 2 (2011): 68. Accessed February 8, 2016. doi:10.3389/fphys.2011.00068.

10. Hergenhahn, B. R. *An Introduction to the History of Psychology.* Belmont: Wadsworth, 2009.

11. Humphrey, Robert. *Stream of Consciousness in the Modern Novel: A Study of James Joyce, Virginia Woolf, Dorothy Richardson, William Faulkner and Others.* Berkeley: University of California Press, 1968.

12. James, Henry, ed. *The Letters of William James.* Boston: Little, Brown & Co, 1926.

13 James, William. "Remarks on Spencer's Definition of Mind as Correspondence." *Journal of Speculative Philosophy* 12, no. 1 (1878): 1–18.

14. ____. *Talks to Teachers on Psychology: And to Students on Some of Life's Ideals.* New York: Henry Holt, 1899.

15. ____. *Pragmatism.* New York: Dover Publications, 1907.

16. ____. *A Pluralistic Universe.* Cambridge, MA: Harvard University Press, 1909.

17. ____. *Essays in Radical Empiricism.* London: Longmans, Green and Co, 1912.

18. ____. *Essays in Philosophy.* Cambridge, MA, and London: Harvard University Press, 1978.

19. ____. *The Will to Believe and Other Essays in Popular Philosophy.* Cambridge, MA, and London: Harvard University Press, 1979.

20. ____. *The Principles of Psychology, Vols 1–2.* Cambridge, MA: Harvard University Press, 1981.

21. ____. *Psychology: Briefer Course.* Cambridge, MA, and London: Harvard University Press, 1984.

22. ____. "The Physical Basis of Emotion." *Psychological Review* 101, no. 2 (1994): 205–10.

23. ____. *The Varieties of Religious Experience.* New York: Barnes and Noble, 2004.

24. Johnson, Michael G., and Tracy B. Henley, eds. *Reflections on* The Principles of Psychology*: William James After a Century.* Hillsdale, NJ: Lawrence Erlbaum Associates, 1990.

25. Pawelski, James. *The Dynamic Individualism of William James.* Albany, NY: State University of New York Press, 2007.

26. Peirce, C. S. *Writings of Charles S. Peirce: A Chronological Edition, Volume 8: 1890–1892.* Peirce Edition Project, 2010.

27. Pope, Kenneth S., and Jerome L. Singer. "Introduction: The Flow of Human Experience." In *The Stream of Consciousness: Scientific Investigations into the Flow of Human Experience*, edited by Kenneth S. Pope and Jerome L. Singer, 1–6. New York: Springer, 1978.

28. Reed, Edward S. *From Soul to Mind: The Emergence of Psychology from Erasmus Darwin to William James.* New Haven, CT: Yale University Press, 1997.

29. Richards, Robert J. "The Personal Equation in Science: William James's Psychological and Moral Uses of the Darwinian Theory." In *A William James Renaissance: Four Essays by Young Scholars*, edited by Mark R. Schwehn. *Harvard Library Bulletin* 30, no. 4 (1982): 387–425.

30. ____. *Pragmatism.* New York: Dover Publications, 1907.

31. ____. *A Pluralistic Universe.* Cambridge, MA: Harvard University Press, 1909.

32. ____. *Essays in Radical Empiricism.* London: Longmans, Green and Co, 1912.

33. ____. *Essays in Philosophy.* Cambridge, MA, and London: Harvard University Press, 1978.

34. ____. *The Will to Believe and Other Essays in Popular Philosophy.* Cambridge, MA, and London: Harvard University Press, 1979.

35. ____. *The Principles of Psychology, Vols 1–2.* Cambridge, MA: Harvard University Press, 1981.

36. ____. *Psychology: Briefer Course.* Cambridge, MA, and London: Harvard University Press, 1984.

37. ____. "The Physical Basis of Emotion." *Psychological Review* 101, no. 2 (1994): 205–10.

38. ____. *The Varieties of Religious Experience.* New York: Barnes and Noble, 2004.

39. Johnson, Michael G., and Tracy B. Henley, eds. *Reflections on* The Principles of Psychology: *William James After a Century.* Hillsdale, NJ: Lawrence Erlbaum Associates, 1990.

40. Pawelski, James. *The Dynamic Individualism of William James.* Albany, NY: State University of New York Press, 2007.

41. Peirce, C. S. *Writings of Charles S. Peirce: A Chronological Edition, Volume 8: 1890–1892.* Peirce Edition Project, 2010.

42. Pope, Kenneth S., and Jerome L. Singer. "Introduction: The Flow of Human Experience." In *The Stream of Consciousness: Scientific Investigations into the Flow of Human Experience,* edited by Kenneth S. Pope and Jerome L. Singer, 1–6. New York: Springer, 1978.

43. Reed, Edward S. *From Soul to Mind: The Emergence of Psychology from Erasmus Darwin to William James.* New Haven, CT: Yale University Press, 1997.

44. Richards, Robert J. "The Personal Equation in Science: William James's Psychological and Moral Uses of the Darwinian Theory." In *A William James Renaissance: Four Essays by Young Scholars,* edited by Mark R. Schwehn. *Harvard Library Bulletin* 30, no. 4 (1982): 387–425.

原书作者简介

威廉·詹姆斯，美国心理学之父，1842 年出生于美国纽约。詹姆斯家境优越，父母非常重视子女教育：在醉心学术前，詹姆斯学过绘画，而他的兄弟亨利则成了一位著名的小说家。1861 年威廉进入哈佛大学劳伦斯科学学院，三年后进入哈佛大学医学院学习医学。学医期间，他曾中断学业，去巴西亚马孙河考察，游历欧洲，并于 1869 年获得了哈佛大学医学学位。1872 年起，詹姆斯任职于哈佛大学，教授生理学和心理学，同时开始撰写他的杰作《心理学原理》。1910 年詹姆斯去世，享年 68 岁。

世界名著中的批判性思维

《世界思想宝库钥匙丛书》致力于深入浅出地阐释全世界著名思想家的观点，不论是谁、在何处都能了解到，从而推进批判性思维发展。

《世界思想宝库钥匙丛书》与世界顶尖大学的一流学者合作，为一系列学科中最有影响的著作推出新的分析文本，介绍其观点和影响。在这一不断扩展的系列中，每种选入的著作都代表了历经时间考验的思想典范。通过为这些著作提供必要背景、揭示原作者的学术渊源以及说明这些著作所产生的影响，本系列图书希望让读者以新视角看待这些划时代的经典之作。读者应学会思考、运用并挑战这些著作中的观点，而不是简单接受它们。

ABOUT THE AUTHOR OF THE ORIGINAL WORK

Born in NewYork City in 1842,"the father of psychology" **William James** grew up in an educated, privileged household. A creative streak ran in the family: William studied painting before settling on a life in academia, while his brother Henry became a well-known novelist. William entered Lawrence Scientific School at Harvard University in 1861 and the university's medical school three years later. After a break to do research in the Amazon and travel in Europe, he completed his medical degree in 1869. He joined the faculty at Harvard in 1872, teaching psychology and philosophy while also writing his masterwork, *The Principles of Psychology*. James died in 1910, aged 68.

ABOUT MACAT
GREAT WORKS FOR CRITICAL THINKING

Macat is focused on making the ideas of the world's great thinkers accessible and comprehensible to everybody, everywhere, in ways that promote the development of enhanced critical thinking skills.

It works with leading academics from the world's top universities to produce new analyses that focus on the ideas and the impact of the most influential works ever written across a wide variety of academic disciplines. Each of the works that sit at the heart of its growing library is an enduring example of great thinking. But by setting them in context—and looking at the influences that shaped their authors, as well as the responses they provoked—Macat encourages readers to look at these classics and game-changers with fresh eyes. Readers learn to think, engage and challenge their ideas, rather than simply accepting them.

批判性思维和《心理学原理》

首要批判性思维技巧：分析
次要批判性思维技巧：创造性思维

1890 年《心理学原理》一经出版便产生了巨大的影响，以致于威廉·詹姆斯被一致认为是心理学之父。尽管在 21 世纪，心理学本身是一门与众不同的学科，但无论是在心理学领域还是在其他领域，詹姆斯的影响从来都是持久而深远的。

从本质上来看，詹姆斯创作的初衷是使《心理学原理》成为心理学这一新兴领域的教科书，对当时心理学已知领域的知识点进行总结和解释。然而，随着时间的推移，《心理学原理》的影响变得越来越深入持久，这要归功于詹姆斯的分析能力和创造性思维。一方面，詹姆斯是一位出色的分析师，他分析心理学的相关知识，探察它们组合的方式，最重要的是，他指出了心理学家知识的不足之处。除此之外，詹姆斯还是一个有创造力的思考者，他从不同的角度看待事物，并提出了许多有创意的解决方案和假设。他最著名的理论有，詹姆斯—兰格理论（一个有关情绪的全新理论）以及"意识流"这一颇具影响的概念，其中"意识流"已经影响了几代心理学家和艺术家。

CRITICAL THINKING AND *THE PRINCIPLES OF PSYCHOLOGY*

• Primary critical thinking skill: ANALYSIS
• Secondary critical thinking skill: CREATIVE THINKING

The impact of William James's 1890 *The Principles of Psychology* is such that he is commonly known as the father of his subject. Though psychology itself is a very different discipline in the 21st-century, James's influence continues to be felt—both within the field and beyond.

At base, *Principles* was designed to be a textbook for what was then an emerging field: a summary and explanation of what was known at that point in time. As its continuing influence shows, though, it became far more—a success due in part to the strength of James's analytical skills and creative thinking. On the one hand, James was a masterful analyst, able to break down what was known in psychology, to trace how it fitted together, and, crucially, to point out the gaps in psychologists' knowledge. Beyond that, though, he was a creative thinker, who looked at things from different angles and proposed inventive solutions and hypotheses. Among his best known was an entirely new theory of emotion (the James-Lange theory), and the influential notion of the "stream of consciousness"—the latter of which has influenced generations of psychologists and artists alike.

《世界思想宝库钥匙丛书》简介

《世界思想宝库钥匙丛书》致力于为一系列在各领域产生重大影响的人文社科类经典著作提供独特的学术探讨。每一本读物都不仅仅是原经典著作的内容摘要，而是介绍并深入研究原经典著作的学术渊源、主要观点和历史影响。这一丛书的目的是提供一套学习资料，以促进读者掌握批判性思维，从而更全面、深刻地去理解重要思想。

每一本读物分为3个部分：学术渊源、学术思想和学术影响，每个部分下有4个小节。这些章节旨在从各个方面研究原经典著作及其反响。

由于独特的体例，每一本读物不但易于阅读，而且另有一项优点：所有读物的编排体例相同，读者在进行某个知识层面的调查或研究时可交叉参阅多本该丛书中的相关读物，从而开启跨领域研究的路径。

为了方便阅读，每本读物最后还列出了术语表和人名表（在书中则以星号＊标记），此外还有参考文献。

《世界思想宝库钥匙丛书》与剑桥大学合作，理清了批判性思维的要点，即如何通过6种技能来进行有效思考。其中3种技能让我们能够理解问题，另3种技能让我们有能力解决问题。这6种技能合称为"批判性思维PACIER模式"，它们是：

分析：了解如何建立一个观点；
评估：研究一个观点的优点和缺点；
阐释：对意义所产生的问题加以理解；
创造性思维：提出新的见解，发现新的联系；
解决问题：提出切实有效的解决办法；
理性化思维：创建有说服力的观点。

THE MACAT LIBRARY

The Macat Library is a series of unique academic explorations of seminal works in the humanities and social sciences — books and papers that have had a significant and widely recognised impact on their disciplines. It has been created to serve as much more than just a summary of what lies between the covers of a great book. It illuminates and explores the influences on, ideas of, and impact of that book. Our goal is to offer a learning resource that encourages critical thinking and fosters a better, deeper understanding of important ideas.

Each publication is divided into three Sections: Influences, Ideas, and Impact. Each Section has four Modules. These explore every important facet of the work, and the responses to it.

This Section-Module structure makes a Macat Library book easy to use, but it has another important feature. Because each Macat book is written to the same format, it is possible (and encouraged!) to cross-reference multiple Macat books along the same lines of inquiry or research. This allows the reader to open up interesting interdisciplinary pathways.

To further aid your reading, lists of glossary terms and people mentioned are included at the end of this book (these are indicated by an asterisk [*] throughout) — as well as a list of works cited.

Macat has worked with the University of Cambridge to identify the elements of critical thinking and understand the ways in which six different skills combine to enable effective thinking.

Three allow us to fully understand a problem; three more give us the tools to solve it. Together, these six skills make up the PACIER model of critical thinking. They are:

ANALYSIS — understanding how an argument is built
EVALUATION — exploring the strengths and weaknesses of an argument
INTERPRETATION — understanding issues of meaning
CREATIVE THINKING — coming up with new ideas and fresh connections
PROBLEM-SOLVING — producing strong solutions
REASONING — creating strong arguments

"《世界思想宝库钥匙丛书》提供了独一无二的跨学科学习和研究工具。它介绍那些革新了各自学科研究的经典著作，还邀请全世界一流专家和教育机构进行严谨的分析，为每位读者打开世界顶级教育的大门。"

—— 安德烈亚斯·施莱歇尔，
经济合作与发展组织教育与技能司司长

"《世界思想宝库钥匙丛书》直面大学教育的巨大挑战……他们组建了一支精干而活跃的学者队伍，来推出在研究广度上颇具新意的教学材料。"

—— 布罗尔斯教授、勋爵，剑桥大学前校长

"《世界思想宝库钥匙丛书》的愿景令人赞叹。它通过分析和阐释那些曾深刻影响人类思想以及社会、经济发展的经典文本，提供了新的学习方法。它推动批判性思维，这对于任何社会和经济体来说都是至关重要的。这就是未来的学习方法。"

—— 查尔斯·克拉克阁下，英国前教育大臣

"对于那些影响了各自领域的著作，《世界思想宝库钥匙丛书》能让人们立即了解到围绕那些著作展开的评论性言论，这让该系列图书成为在这些领域从事研究的师生们不可或缺的资源。"

—— 威廉·特朗佐教授，加利福尼亚大学圣地亚哥分校

"Macat offers an amazing first-of-its-kind tool for interdisciplinary learning and research. Its focus on works that transformed their disciplines and its rigorous approach, drawing on the world's leading experts and educational institutions, opens up a world-class education to anyone."

—— Andreas Schleicher, Director for Education and Skills,
Organisation for Economic Co-operation and Development

"Macat is taking on some of the major challenges in university education... They have drawn together a strong team of active academics who are producing teaching materials that are novel in the breadth of their approach."

—— Prof Lord Broers, former Vice-Chancellor of the University of Cambridge

"The Macat vision is exceptionally exciting. It focuses upon new modes of learning which analyse and explain seminal texts which have profoundly influenced world thinking and so social and economic development. It promotes the kind of critical thinking which is essential for any society and economy. This is the learning of the future."

—— Rt Hon Charles Clarke, former UK Secretary of State for Education

"The Macat analyses provide immediate access to the critical conversation surrounding the books that have shaped their respective discipline, which will make them an invaluable resource to all of those, students and teachers, working in the field."

—— Prof William Tronzo, University of California at San Diego

TITLE	中文书名	类别
An Analysis of Arjun Appadurai's *Modernity at Large: Cultural Dimensions of Globalization*	解析阿尔君·阿帕杜莱《消失的现代性：全球化的文化维度》	人类学
An Analysis of Claude Lévi-Strauss's *Structural Anthropology*	解析克劳德·列维-斯特劳斯《结构人类学》	人类学
An Analysis of Marcel Mauss's *The Gift*	解析马塞尔·莫斯《礼物》	人类学
An Analysis of Jared M. Diamond's *Guns, Germs, and Steel: The Fate of Human Societies*	解析贾雷德·M.戴蒙德《枪炮、病菌与钢铁：人类社会的命运》	人类学
An Analysis of Clifford Geertz's *The Interpretation of Cultures*	解析克利福德·格尔茨《文化的解释》	人类学
An Analysis of Philippe Ariès's *Centuries of Childhood: A Social History of Family Life*	解析菲力浦·阿利埃斯《儿童的世纪：旧制度下的儿童和家庭生活》	人类学
An Analysis of W. Chan Kim & Renée Mauborgne's *Blue Ocean Strategy*	解析金伟灿/勒妮·莫博涅《蓝海战略》	商业
An Analysis of John P. Kotter's *Leading Change*	解析约翰·P.科特《领导变革》	商业
An Analysis of Michael E. Porter's *Competitive Strategy: Techniques for Analyzing Industries and Competitors*	解析迈克尔·E.波特《竞争战略：分析产业和竞争对手的技术》	商业
An Analysis of Jean Lave & Etienne Wenger's *Situated Learning: Legitimate Peripheral Participation*	解析琼·莱夫/艾蒂纳·温格《情境学习：合法的边缘性参与》	商业
An Analysis of Douglas McGregor's *The Human Side of Enterprise*	解析道格拉斯·麦格雷戈《企业的人性面》	商业
An Analysis of Milton Friedman's *Capitalism and Freedom*	解析米尔顿·弗里德曼《资本主义与自由》	商业
An Analysis of Ludwig von Mises's *The Theory of Money and Credit*	解析路德维希·冯·米塞斯《货币和信用理论》	经济学
An Analysis of Adam Smith's *The Wealth of Nations*	解析亚当·斯密《国富论》	经济学
An Analysis of Thomas Piketty's *Capital in the Twenty-First Century*	解析托马斯·皮凯蒂《21世纪资本论》	经济学
An Analysis of Nassim Nicholas Taleb's *The Black Swan: The Impact of the Highly Improbable*	解析纳西姆·尼古拉斯·塔勒布《黑天鹅：如何应对不可预知的未来》	经济学
An Analysis of Ha-Joon Chang's *Kicking Away the Ladder*	解析张夏准《富国陷阱：发达国家为何踢开梯子》	经济学
An Analysis of Thomas Robert Malthus's *An Essay on the Principle of Population*	解析托马斯·罗伯特·马尔萨斯《人口论》	经济学

An Analysis of John Maynard Keynes's *The General Theory of Employment, Interest and Money*	解析约翰·梅纳德·凯恩斯《就业、利息和货币通论》	经济学
An Analysis of Milton Friedman's *The Role of Monetary Policy*	解析米尔顿·弗里德曼《货币政策的作用》	经济学
An Analysis of Burton G. Malkiel's *A Random Walk Down Wall Street*	解析伯顿·G. 马尔基尔《漫步华尔街》	经济学
An Analysis of Friedrich A. Hayek's *The Road to Serfdom*	解析弗里德里希·A. 哈耶克《通往奴役之路》	经济学
An Analysis of Charles P. Kindleberger's *Manias, Panics, and Crashes: A History of Financial Crises*	解析查尔斯·P. 金德尔伯格《疯狂、惊恐和崩溃：金融危机史》	经济学
An Analysis of Amartya Sen's *Development as Freedom*	解析阿马蒂亚·森《以自由看待发展》	经济学
An Analysis of Rachel Carson's *Silent Spring*	解析蕾切尔·卡森《寂静的春天》	地理学
An Analysis of Charles Darwin's *On the Origin of Species: by Means of Natural Selection, or The Preservation of Favoured Races in the Struggle for Life*	解析查尔斯·达尔文《物种起源》	地理学
An Analysis of World Commission on Environment and Development's *The Brundtland Report, Our Common Future*	解析世界环境与发展委员会《布伦特兰报告：我们共同的未来》	地理学
An Analysis of James E. Lovelock's *Gaia: A New Look at Life on Earth*	解析詹姆斯·E. 拉伍洛克《盖娅：地球生命的新视野》	地理学
An Analysis of Paul Kennedy's *The Rise and Fall of the Great Powers: Economic Change and Military Conflict from 1500—2000*	解析保罗·肯尼迪《大国的兴衰：1500—2000 年的经济变革与军事冲突》	历史
An Analysis of Janet L. Abu-Lughod's *Before European Hegemony: The World System A. D. 1250—1350*	解析珍妮特·L. 阿布-卢格霍德《欧洲霸权之前：1250—1350 年的世界体系》	历史
An Analysis of Alfred W. Crosby's *The Columbian Exchange: Biological and Cultural Consequences of 1492*	解析艾尔弗雷德·W. 克罗斯比《哥伦布大交换：1492 年以后的生物影响和文化冲击》	历史
An Analysis of Tony Judt's *Postwar: A History of Europe since 1945*	解析托尼·朱特《战后欧洲史》	历史
An Analysis of Richard J. Evans's *In Defence of History*	解析理查德·J. 艾文斯《捍卫历史》	历史
An Analysis of Eric Hobsbawm's *The Age of Revolution: Europe 1789–1848*	解析艾瑞克·霍布斯鲍姆《革命的年代：欧洲 1789—1848 年》	历史

An Analysis of Roland Barthes's *Mythologies*	解析罗兰·巴特《神话学》	文学与批判理论
An Analysis of Simone de Beauvoir's *The Second Sex*	解析西蒙娜·德·波伏娃《第二性》	文学与批判理论
An Analysis of Edward W. Said's *Orientalism*	解析爱德华·W. 萨义德《东方主义》	文学与批判理论
An Analysis of Virginia Woolf's *A Room of One's Own*	解析弗吉尼亚·伍尔芙《一间自己的房间》	文学与批判理论
An Analysis of Judith Butler's *Gender Trouble*	解析朱迪斯·巴特勒《性别麻烦》	文学与批判理论
An Analysis of Ferdinand de Saussure's *Course in General Linguistics*	解析费尔迪南·德·索绪尔《普通语言学教程》	文学与批判理论
An Analysis of Susan Sontag's *On Photography*	解析苏珊·桑塔格《论摄影》	文学与批判理论
An Analysis of Walter Benjamin's *The Work of Art in the Age of Mechanical Reproduction*	解析瓦尔特·本雅明《机械复制时代的艺术作品》	文学与批判理论
An Analysis of W.E.B. Du Bois's *The Souls of Black Folk*	解析 W.E.B. 杜波依斯《黑人的灵魂》	文学与批判理论
An Analysis of Plato's *The Republic*	解析柏拉图《理想国》	哲学
An Analysis of Plato's *Symposium*	解析柏拉图《会饮篇》	哲学
An Analysis of Aristotle's *Metaphysics*	解析亚里士多德《形而上学》	哲学
An Analysis of Aristotle's *Nicomachean Ethics*	解析亚里士多德《尼各马可伦理学》	哲学
An Analysis of Immanuel Kant's *Critique of Pure Reason*	解析伊曼努尔·康德《纯粹理性批判》	哲学
An Analysis of Ludwig Wittgenstein's *Philosophical Investigations*	解析路德维希·维特根斯坦《哲学研究》	哲学
An Analysis of G.W.F. Hegel's *Phenomenology of Spirit*	解析 G.W.F. 黑格尔《精神现象学》	哲学
An Analysis of Baruch Spinoza's *Ethics*	解析巴鲁赫·斯宾诺莎《伦理学》	哲学
An Analysis of Hannah Arendt's *The Human Condition*	解析汉娜·阿伦特《人的境况》	哲学
An Analysis of G.E.M. Anscombe's *Modern Moral Philosophy*	解析 G.E.M. 安斯康姆《现代道德哲学》	哲学
An Analysis of David Hume's *An Enquiry Concerning Human Understanding*	解析大卫·休谟《人类理解研究》	哲学

An Analysis of Søren Kierkegaard's *Fear and Trembling*	解析索伦·克尔凯郭尔《恐惧与战栗》	哲学
An Analysis of René Descartes's *Meditations on First Philosophy*	解析勒内·笛卡尔《第一哲学沉思录》	哲学
An Analysis of Friedrich Nietzsche's *On the Genealogy of Morality*	解析弗里德里希·尼采《论道德的谱系》	哲学
An Analysis of Gilbert Ryle's *The Concept of Mind*	解析吉尔伯特·赖尔《心的概念》	哲学
An Analysis of Thomas Kuhn's *The Structure of Scientific Revolutions*	解析托马斯·库恩《科学革命的结构》	哲学
An Analysis of John Stuart Mill's *Utilitarianism*	解析约翰·斯图亚特·穆勒《功利主义》	哲学
An Analysis of Aristotle's *Politics*	解析亚里士多德《政治学》	政治学
An Analysis of Niccolò Machiavelli's *The Prince*	解析尼科洛·马基雅维利《君主论》	政治学
An Analysis of Karl Marx's *Capital*	解析卡尔·马克思《资本论》	政治学
An Analysis of Benedict Anderson's *Imagined Communities*	解析本尼迪克特·安德森《想象的共同体》	政治学
An Analysis of Samuel P. Huntington's *The Clash of Civilizations and the Remaking of World Order*	解析塞缪尔·P.亨廷顿《文明的冲突与世界秩序的重建》	政治学
An Analysis of Alexis de Tocqueville's *Democracy in America*	解析阿列克西·德·托克维尔《论美国的民主》	政治学
An Analysis of John A. Hobson's *Imperialism: A Study*	解析约翰·A.霍布森《帝国主义》	政治学
An Analysis of Thomas Paine's *Common Sense*	解析托马斯·潘恩《常识》	政治学
An Analysis of John Rawls's *A Theory of Justice*	解析约翰·罗尔斯《正义论》	政治学
An Analysis of Francis Fukuyama's *The End of History and the Last Man*	解析弗朗西斯·福山《历史的终结与最后的人》	政治学
An Analysis of John Locke's *Two Treatises of Government*	解析约翰·洛克《政府论》	政治学
An Analysis of Sun Tzu's *The Art of War*	解析孙武《孙子兵法》	政治学
An Analysis of Henry Kissinger's *World Order: Reflections on the Character of Nations and the Course of History*	解析亨利·基辛格《世界秩序》	政治学
An Analysis of Jean-Jacques Rousseau's *The Social Contract*	解析让-雅克·卢梭《社会契约论》	政治学

An Analysis of Odd Arne Westad's *The Global Cold War: Third World Interventions and the Making of Our Times*	解析文安立《全球冷战：美苏对第三世界的干涉与当代世界的形成》	政治学
An Analysis of Sigmund Freud's *The Interpretation of Dreams*	解析西格蒙德·弗洛伊德《梦的解析》	心理学
An Analysis of William James' *The Principles of Psychology*	解析威廉·詹姆斯《心理学原理》	心理学
An Analysis of Philip Zimbardo's *The Lucifer Effect*	解析菲利普·津巴多《路西法效应》	心理学
An Analysis of Leon Festinger's *A Theory of Cognitive Dissonance*	解析利昂·费斯汀格《认知失调论》	心理学
An Analysis of Richard H. Thaler & Cass R. Sunstein's *Nudge: Improving Decisions about Health, Wealth, and Happiness*	解析理查德·H. 泰勒／卡斯·R. 桑斯坦《助推：如何做出有关健康、财富和幸福的更优决策》	心理学
An Analysis of Gordon Allport's *The Nature of Prejudice*	解析高尔登·奥尔波特《偏见的本质》	心理学
An Analysis of Steven Pinker's *The Better Angels of Our Nature: Why Violence Has Declined*	解析斯蒂芬·平克《人性中的善良天使：暴力为什么会减少》	心理学
An Analysis of Stanley Milgram's *Obedience to Authority*	解析斯坦利·米尔格拉姆《对权威的服从》	心理学
An Analysis of Betty Friedan's *The Feminine Mystique*	解析贝蒂·弗里丹《女性的奥秘》	心理学
An Analysis of David Riesman's *The Lonely Crowd: A Study of the Changing American Character*	解析大卫·理斯曼《孤独的人群：美国人社会性格演变之研究》	社会学
An Analysis of Franz Boas's *Race, Language and Culture*	解析弗朗兹·博厄斯《种族、语言与文化》	社会学
An Analysis of Pierre Bourdieu's *Outline of a Theory of Practice*	解析皮埃尔·布尔迪厄《实践理论大纲》	社会学
An Analysis of Max Weber's *The Protestant Ethic and the Spirit of Capitalism*	解析马克斯·韦伯《新教伦理与资本主义精神》	社会学
An Analysis of Jane Jacobs's *The Death and Life of Great American Cities*	解析简·雅各布斯《美国大城市的死与生》	社会学
An Analysis of C. Wright Mills's *The Sociological Imagination*	解析 C. 赖特·米尔斯《社会学的想象力》	社会学
An Analysis of Robert E. Lucas Jr.'s *Why Doesn't Capital Flow from Rich to Poor Countries?*	解析小罗伯特·E. 卢卡斯《为何资本不从富国流向穷国？》	社会学

An Analysis of Émile Durkheim's *On Suicide*	解析埃米尔·迪尔凯姆《自杀论》	社会学
An Analysis of Eric Hoffer's *The True Believer: Thoughts on the Nature of Mass Movements*	解析埃里克·霍弗《狂热分子：群众运动圣经》	社会学
An Analysis of Jared M. Diamond's *Collapse: How Societies Choose to Fail or Survive*	解析贾雷德·M.戴蒙德《大崩溃：社会如何选择兴亡》	社会学
An Analysis of Michel Foucault's *The History of Sexuality Vol. 1: The Will to Knowledge*	解析米歇尔·福柯《性史（第一卷）：求知意志》	社会学
An Analysis of Michel Foucault's *Discipline and Punish*	解析米歇尔·福柯《规训与惩罚》	社会学
An Analysis of Richard Dawkins's *The Selfish Gene*	解析理查德·道金斯《自私的基因》	社会学
An Analysis of Antonio Gramsci's *Prison Notebooks*	解析安东尼奥·葛兰西《狱中札记》	社会学
An Analysis of Augustine's *Confessions*	解析奥古斯丁《忏悔录》	神学
An Analysis of C. S. Lewis's *The Abolition of Man*	解析 C. S. 路易斯《人之废》	神学

图书在版编目（CIP）数据

解析威廉·詹姆斯《心理学原理》：汉、英 / 英国Macat出版社团队著；叶娟译.
—上海：上海外语教育出版社，2019
（世界思想宝库钥匙丛书）
ISBN 978-7-5446-5993-2

Ⅰ.①解… Ⅱ.①英… ②叶… Ⅲ.①詹姆斯（James, William 1842—1910）—心理学—研究—汉、英 Ⅳ.①B712.44

中国版本图书馆CIP数据核字（2019）第175497号

This Chinese-English bilingual edition of *An Analysis of William James's* The Principles of Psychology is published by arrangement with Macat International Limited.
Licensed for sale throughout the world.
本书汉英双语版由Macat国际有限公司授权上海外语教育出版社有限公司出版。
供在全世界范围内发行、销售。

图字：09－2018－549

出版发行：上海外语教育出版社
　　　　　　　（上海外国语大学内）　邮编：200083
电　　话： 021-65425300（总机）
电子邮箱： bookinfo@sflep.com.cn
网　　址： http://www.sflep.com
责任编辑： 王叶涵

印　　刷： 上海信老印刷厂
开　　本： 890×1240　1/32　印张 5.25　字数 109千字
版　　次： 2020 年 6 月第 1 版　　2020 年 6 月第 1 次印刷
印　　数： 2 100 册

书　　号： ISBN 978-7-5446-5993-2
定　　价： 30.00 元
　　　本版图书如有印装质量问题，可向本社调换
　　　质量服务热线：4008-213-263　电子邮箱：editorial@sflep.com